FOOLPROOF

THE ART OF COMMUNICATION FOR LAWYERS AND PROFESSIONALS

Foolproof

The Art of Communication for Lawyers and Professionals

Rebecca Diaz-Bonilla

NATIONAL INSTITUTE FOR TRIAL ADVOCACY

Address inquiries to:

Reprint Permission
National Institute for Trial Advocacy
1685 38th Street, Suite 200
Boulder, CO 80301-2735
Phone: (800) 225-6482
Fax: (720) 890-7069
Email: permissions@nita.org

Library of Congress Cataloging-in-Publication Data

Names: Diaz-Bonilla, Rebecca, author.

Title: Foolproof : the art of communication for lawyers and professionals / Rebecca Diaz-Bonilla.

Description: Second edition. | Boulder, CO : National Institute for Trial Advocacy, [2018] | Includes index.

Identifiers: LCCN 2018015721 (print) | LCCN 2018017331 (ebook) | ISBN 9781601567949 (ebook) | ISBN 9781601567932 | ISBN 9781601567949 (eISBN)

Subjects: LCSH: Forensic oratory. | Oral communication. | Communication in law. | Lawyers--Handbooks, manuals, etc.

Classification: LCC K181 (ebook) | LCC K181 .D53 2018 (print) | DDC

340/.14--dc23

LC record available at https://lccn.loc.gov/2018015721

ISBN 978-1-60156-793-2
eISBN 978-1-60156-794-9
FBA 1793

Printed in the United States.

This book is dedicated to my devoted parents,
to my incredible children,
and to my beloved husband.
Soli Deo Gloria.

CONTENTS

Chapter Four: Voice/Speech Basics—Posture, Breath, Sound, and Quality

CONTRIBUTIONS

I would like to thank my husband, Mariano, and my mother and father, Carolyn and Daniel McCormack, for all their encouragement and help creating this book. I would also like to thank the following people for their contributions: John Baker, Megan Bellamy, Michelle Blake, James Brosnahan, Kristen Bucher, Kate Burke, Robert Chapel, Doris Cheng, Michael Dale, Mariano Diaz-Bonilla, Victoria Diaz-Bonilla, Michael Howard, Vickie Kobak, Peter Lyons, Robert Sayler, Kenneth Svendsen, Angela Vita, Judge Nancy Vaidik, Frank Vlossak, and Richard Warner.

CHAPTER ONE

THE LOST ART OF RHETORIC AND HOW TO FIND IT

"Defeat? I do not recognise the meaning of the word."

—*Margaret Thatcher*

Things seem harder today than they used to be. The Information Age may bring kilobytes of information to our fingertips, but the path forward is often unclear. Information is no longer a differentiator; rather, it's what you *do* with information— how you communicate it—that makes you stand out. This paralyzing volume of information exposes a gap in the legal market: few attorneys are capable of digesting all the data and crafting simple and compelling arguments or presentations that sway others to follow their lead. The demand for the skill of persuasion is at a premium.

Being a lawyer is harder. Obtaining clients, convincing them of the merits of a case, and persuading the other side have all become more difficult. Taking the lead on a call, emerging as the expert in a meeting, and showing charisma during a presentation is harder. In all practice areas—contract, government, arbitration, bankruptcy, reorganization, real estate, securities, corporate, banking and finance, venture, and litigation—the competition is stiffer.

So what can you do to tip the scales in your favor? What can you do to make your advice memorable? What can you do to take command of a room or lead a call effectively? What will compel a potential client to hire you, convince the other contracting party to take a reasonable offer, or persuade a jury or arbitrator to give your preferred verdict or decision?

Clients want professionals with deep subject-matter expertise and experience, but they hire individuals who can explain and persuade. An attorney needs to be competent, of course, but she must also be able to persuade the client to trust her. To excel professionally (and even personally), attorneys must be able to persuade. To do this successfully, attorneys need excellent oral communication skills. Do you have the oral communication skills necessary to tip the scale?

Oral communication, also known as rhetoric, is the art of persuasive speaking or writing. It includes every word communicated to any audience using any medium or technology. Your personal and professional day is filled with oral communication:

phone calls, client meetings, pitches, lunches, lectures, leadership opportunities, chats with support staff, formal speeches, conversations with family and friends, and everything in between.

Oral communication also includes what you don't say: words left unspoken, pauses that seem eternal, hesitations that break a rhythm. These, if perfected, can deliver exactly the right emphasis or message without you ever making a sound. In its broadest interpretation, oral communication also includes your body language. Your facial expression and eye contact, movement, and posture can communicate a message just as effectively as the spoken word.

The goal of oral communication training is to give you skills that coupled with your expertise and experience will help you explain a complex matter or persuade even the most difficult audience of the legitimacy of your position. The skills that you will learn will help you craft arguments that appeal to the widest possible variety of audiences without sacrificing your individuality. In oral communication, certain behaviors, mannerisms, and styles can offend, while others can appeal to audiences. Together, we will shed those that do not appeal and develop the appropriate techniques. This book is a manual for improvement, written as though you and I were sitting across the table from one another. Together we will:

- review the theory and practical application of oral communication;

- assess your skills and identify areas where you can improve;

- develop an improvement plan; and

- take the steps—including practice exercises that you will do while you work through this book—to make you more effective at oral communication and emerge as a leader.

I am writing for all attorneys, not just those who go to court. Whether you negotiate contracts, close mergers and acquisitions, or appear at zoning hearings, your effort to persuade is as critical to your success as it is for a litigator trying to sway the jury.

1.1 How We Lost Our Voice

A few years ago, I stumbled on a grammar school report card from the 1920s. I opened it and found my subject matter staring at me—*elocution*, the art of clear and expressive public speaking with an emphasis on gesture, vocal production, delivery, and distinct pronunciation and articulation. Unfortunately for lawyers today, elocution training is absent in most grammar, middle, or high schools. Most colleges and universities do not require courses in public speaking or oral examinations. No longer extant are the debating societies and organizations like the Young Men's Lyceum in Springfield, Illinois, which helped a young Lincoln polish his oral presentation skills.

When students arrive at law school, not only do they have little foundation on which to build, but there is also little training available in the law school curricula. Unaware of the benefits gained from mastering these skills—or as a coping mechanism for little to no instruction—attorneys ignore developing oral communication, or worse, form bad habits. Neither works well. It is daunting to require a practicing attorney, tasked with billing infinite hours, to find the time to remediate bad habits that have been unknowingly formed for over two decades. Yet I have witnessed the successful results of such efforts.

In law school, students take courses in legal writing, enter writing competitions, and write briefs for moot court or articles for law review. Law professors also grade and critique their students' written work at the end of every semester. While most law schools still employ the Socratic method of teaching, hold moot court competitions, and offer trial advocacy courses, they offer few courses that focus on oral advocacy and most are not required. As a result, most law school graduates are better prepared for written communication than oral communication. In law firms, young attorneys write papers, contracts, letters, bills, emails, and pleadings. In practice, a partner usually reviews an associate's written work product. There is no parallel path for oral communication training.

In this book, I discuss the differences between legal writing and the writing style best suited to prepare an oral presentation. I wrote this book in a user-friendly style so you become accustomed to a more casual style of expression. Shut the door to your office, and participate actively in the exercises as they appear. Try reading the book aloud, and learn these lost skills through lessons from the performing arts.

1.2   All Attorneys Need Strong Oral Communication Skills

In over a decade of coaching, I repeatedly heard the same misconception: only litigators need to communicate well. How false! Oral communication is not just for litigators—all lawyers use oral communication.

Communication is at the heart of the legal profession. A lawyer's expertise and experience create the content that he communicates orally and in writing. Since lawyers are advocates for their clients, much of the communication is intended to inform, educate, and, most importantly, persuade. When lawyers are good at oral communication—when they can explain and persuade—they become better leaders. The better they are as leaders, the better equipped they will be to lead in a variety of situations: a process for a client, a team that needs to close a deal, a firm or professional organization, or a community organization.

In critical situations—when persuading someone was crucial to getting the client, settling a contract dispute before it exploded, or negotiating a major acquisition—how many times have you wished you could speak with a key person rather than send an email, a letter, or a position paper?

Oral communication is more powerful and efficient. There are more senses involved in persuasion. The other side hears you and, if you are present, sees you. You can read the person's reaction as you speak and determine if you are connecting. If you're not persuading but are nimble and skillful, you can make the necessary change to ensure the presentation is a success. Yet we ignore communication skills, fail to assess them, and avoid opportunities for training. If you can learn these communication skills, you improve your ability to effectively and persuasively use oral communication to advance your career, personal and professional goals, and reputation.

In addition to providing sound counsel, lawyers need to build and maintain relationships with clients, colleagues, the judiciary, and other members of the profession. They must continually sell themselves and their skill set in the market place. Oral communication skills have a broad and important impact on a successful career. I have experienced it many times over—a young associate focuses energy on writing, becomes a senior associate who writes well, and then one day calls me in a panic after an embarrassing meeting exposed his shortfall in oral communication skills. The tide abruptly shifts, and this associate's future at the firm looks bleak because of faded or nonexistent oral communication skills. Don't despair if this seems familiar; I have witnessed successful comebacks for those willing to dedicate the time and effort to improve.

1.3   What Makes Me an Expert?

Simply put, I work at it every day. Like you, to be successful I work at, build, and practice oral communication skills. My journey in communications training began on the stage. I am not a speech therapist, psychologist, or communications major. I'm an attorney with an undergraduate major in drama. I am, and have always been, a performer.

From childhood, I studied, practiced, and trained in voice, acting, and movement; I loved to sing, dance, act, and play the piano. I performed in regional theater, studied in New York, and eventually graduated from the University of Virginia with an acting degree. I excelled at every level of theater and received the highest awards and accolades; however, at the time, I did not realize the value of my training, practice, and education in the performing arts. At law school, I noticed some of the brightest members of my class failed to shine when presenting in study group sessions or in front of the class. As with other law schools now and then, there was little or no training in oral communication. I did not know at the time that a few years later I would set out to fill this gap in the market.

After graduating from the University of Virginia, I entered law school. I worked at a lobbying law firm to pay for school, and after graduation I joined a law firm as a litigator. On each step of the ladder, my illusions about the eloquence of attorneys continued to dissolve. It was clear that attorneys needed training in performing, irrespective of the audience size. I'm not just picking on attorneys, however. They are not the only ones unprepared in the art of communicating. In fact, members of most professions are woefully unprepared in oral communication skills.

After practicing in Virginia, I embraced motherhood, moved to New York with my husband, and began raising our family. A few years later, I returned to the University of Virginia, where Robert Sayler of Covington & Burling LLC asked me to co-teach oral advocacy classes at the University of Virginia School of Law. We wrote courses on oral advocacy for litigators and nonlitigators and taught together for several semesters. When my family moved again, I helped transition my replacement at the law school and launched a consulting business teaching communication skills to practicing attorneys.

Over the past decade, I have worked all over the world, with law firms of every size and attorneys of every experience level, across most practice areas (including corporate, regulatory, transactional, and litigation), and with legal associations in the United States and Europe. Here is what I have observed: attorneys do not receive sufficient training in oral communication.

- Training in oral presentation skills is seen as remedial, rather than as a valuable tool for all.

- Attorneys need focused oral presentation skills training to be successful in all aspects of their practice—whether pitching new clients, explaining a new securities regulation, or arguing in traffic court.

- Most attorneys misperceive their oral communication capabilities.

- Oral presentation behaviors are personal and can develop into good or bad habits.

- Successful attorneys have great communication skills.

Professional development experts track the same trends and know the value of oral communications training for attorneys:

> One of the misconceptions many lawyers have is that oral advocacy and presentation skills training is remedial. In other fields in which professionals speak publicly to inform and persuade, this training is coveted. It is a prerequisite for politicians and television journalists, and a perk for senior executives and leaders in philanthropy. Those most talented seek training to further develop their skills. On the other hand, lawyers, whose roles are to inform and persuade, get very little training in the "oral" of oral advocacy. Law schools teach legal analysis, persuasive writing, and advocacy procedures. Law schools provide an opportunity to apply these in moot court or in a clinic. But very few law schools have experts who provide individual feedback and teach established oral communication techniques. And integrated feedback and practiced techniques are

essential to hone the art and craft of effective, dynamic oral advocacy. By providing oral advocacy and presentation skills training to our lawyers, we raise the bar (pun intended!) for effective, dynamic client service.

(Vickie Germain Kobak, Professional Development Consultant).

1.4 Ancient Rhetoric

Before we get to work, some background about rhetoric and oral communication will help build a foundation to support our task ahead.

Oral communication skills were taught in ancient times. The Greeks and Romans understood the importance of oral communication. Aristotle heralded a clear and accurate understanding of good rhetoric. Without printing presses and computers, oral presentation skill was critical in ancient Greece. Without these skills, a young man in Athens would never achieve success or be well regarded. Aristotle defined rhetoric as the discovery of the available means of persuasion and explained how to assess the success of a rhetorician through the metrics of ethos, pathos, and logos:

- ethos—manifestation of good character;
- pathos—excitement of the emotions; and
- logos—excitement of the mind with reason.

If that sounds like "Greek" to you, here's the translation:

- If people generally trust and rely on you, you may have a good level of ethos. We believe people we *respect*.

- If you've been complimented for how you bring enthusiasm to a room or sway an audience to empathize with your cause, you may have a high degree of pathos. We persuade not just with reason but also by appealing to the audience's *emotions*.

- If professors and/or senior lawyers praise you for clear, cogent thinking, you may display good logos. We like to see the *reason* in an argument before accepting it.

Remember these terms: ethos, pathos, and logos. Aristotle understood oral communication well, and I will refer back to these principles as we work on your rhetoric.

Cicero, Rome's greatest orator and prose stylist, later expanded on Aristotle's thoughts on rhetoric by setting clear guidelines for orators. Cicero taught:

1. Know the subject. Without this, oral communication is windy verbiage.

2. Choose words well and arrange them cleverly.

3. Understand emotions and how they can be calmed or excited by what you say and how you say it.

4. Delivery conveys and changes meaning. Delivery includes timing, pauses, and rhythm; it also includes physical deportment, which includes not only hand, arm, and head movement, but also gestures, facial expression, and voice production—and an understanding of the need to avoid monotony.

5. Practice (Cicero thought reciting poetry was an exceptional exercise).

6. Be in shape. Practice breath control. Oration is physical work.

I couldn't agree more with Cicero. His teachings are just as relevant today as in ancient Rome, and I will rely heavily on these principles throughout the book. We will evaluate your skills in chapter two and discover where you are weakest within Cicero's framework of preparation and delivery, and then work toward improving.

1.5 Oral Communication in a Digital Age

You must be proactive, not reactive, to improve your oral communication skills effectively. Too often we identify the need for self-improvement as a counteraction to the most recent calamity (the "great recession," for example) or hottest technological trend (social media). To be sure, these events and trends can be an alarm to invest in oral communication skills—after all, oral communication skills certainly do not improve with tweeting and texting. However, the decline in oral communication training over the last fifty years has left most practicing attorneys—even those whose careers began before the digital age—at a competitive disadvantage to those few attorneys who, with equal experience and expertise, had training (or a natural ability) in oral communication.

The advent of digital communication, including social media, has starved many attorneys of the usual or necessary remaining outlets for practicing good oral communication skills. As social media numbs another generation of attorneys to these needed skills, training in oral communications is more than ever before an indispensable asset. Law firms and bar associations have begun to invest in more communication training for associates—and even partners. The profession, not just those who litigate, acknowledges that improving communication skills can be a competitive advantage that adds to the bottom line. The growing demand from law firms and individual attorneys for my consulting services demonstrates a renewed focus on strengthening oral communication and presentation skills.

1.6 Sensitivity: An Obstacle to Learning

Clients tell me that I am "brutal, but fair" in my coaching. The "brutal" part comes from studying acting. Directors sometimes have to deliver honest criticism in nerve-racking, vulnerable situations. Acting teachers and directors deliver honest (sometimes seen as brutal) feedback without much regard for particular sensitivities. Honest feedback creates a ripe environment for improvement. While most agree that honest critique helps you improve, I often encounter attorneys who have never received an honest assessment of their strengths and weaknesses in oral communications.

In this book, I share techniques for improvement based on my experience and training. Some attorneys may be turned off that I use acting techniques to teach oral communication skills. They will think, "But we're not actors." Some feel that such training reinforces perceptions that lawyers are tricksters, manipulating jurors with fast talk and slight-of-hand techniques—i.e., actors. My advice? Drop the sensitivity. It's only the content of the message that's different, not the techniques for good delivery. You need to do your part: 1) accept advice with an open mind and a willingness to grow, and 2) implement the techniques within your professional and personal lives. As part of the self-assessment you need to move forward, ask a colleague or friend to observe you during the next meeting or conference call, and request feedback on your "performance" based on the techniques presented in this book. Ask your observer to be frank, even be brutal if you have thick skin and an open mind! Don't become discouraged—voice, body language, and emotional improvements are hard to achieve in self-study. The legal marketplace is continuously flooded with information and grows more and more competitive every day, but this book provides you with the foundation on which you can build and improve.

Chapter Two

Where Does Improvement Begin?

"All things are difficult before they are easy."

—*Thomas Fuller*

Now that you understand the goal of this book as well as the importance and benefits of improving your communication skills, let me define a few terms and phrases that we'll be using as we turn to assessing your current skills.

Rhetoric is an art, so teachers may use terms differently. We need to communicate using the same vocabulary. When I mention *oral communication,* I refer to phone calls, conversations, small group meetings, lectures, panels, large presentations, and everything in between. For our use, *audience* means anyone listening or present when you open your mouth to speak or participate in a conversation or meeting. An "audience" might be one person on a phone call or a ballroom full of listeners. A *presentation* or *performance* is an oral communication delivered in any context. *"Elements of style" or "style"* include how you use or show voice or speech pattern, body language, emotion, and dynamics.

In this chapter, you will take a brief self-assessment so you acquire a realistic understanding of where you currently stand. Next, you will be exposed to the "big picture" of improvement: set goals, write, rehearse, and perform.

2.1   How to Assess Your Skills

As an attorney, you are busy. You need identifiable, measurable goals as well as a timeline for achieving landmarks in developing any skill set. The same is true with improving oral presentation skills. Feedback and constructive criticism are valuable when they help you achieve realistic and measurable goals. If I met with you in person, I would assess your skills and work with you to set goals. Using this book, you will make a self-assessment (with the help of a friend or colleague), and rely on your review of audio and video recordings for immediate feedback.

I haven't met two attorneys who needed the exact same coaching. Oral communication skills are personal. Some attorneys excel on the telephone; some thrive off-script; others need a formal PowerPoint to feel comfortable; a few read a typed word-for-word script. Some attorneys enjoy big crowds; others prefer one-on-one encounters. Oral communication skills can be applied and crafted for each setting. Sometimes attorneys assess themselves and their skill level without fully understanding the techniques or without the honesty that an objective observer can offer. I will help you self-assess your strengths and weaknesses. Having some outside input is useful. If possible, ask a forthright friend or colleague to help you with the assessment so you can capture a clear picture of the current state of your skills. This friend or colleague can also play a helpful role in the practice exercises I offer in this book. I've included tables for you and your colleague to use. With the assessment, you can set reasonable goals for improvement. Just like a closing checklist for a deal, you can use these tables as checklists to focus on the weaknesses in your oral communication skills.

I evaluate a client using all of the following methods:

- Aristotle and Cicero—Classic Rhetoric.

- Personal Description.

- Scenario Rankings.

The first gives a big-picture view of your skills in general. The next two evaluations help narrow goals and identify areas for improvement. Each gives a different insight on how you can improve.

As you assess your current communications skill level, keep in mind that every presentation is not the same and results can change with different variables, including audience size, posture (e.g., seated or standing), audience profile (e.g., friend or foe; superior, peer, or subordinate), and environment (e.g., lunch, conference room, courtroom, etc.). Adrenaline also triggers nerves for attorneys in different ways. Some get empowered; others get scared. Remember, this is an art, not a science. Don't expect a right answer as you would find in calculus. Also, as you read and make a self-assessment, take note of patterns in the way you have been communicating. For example, do you sometimes lose your train of thought when called on unexpectedly in a meeting? Do you succeed in a question-and-answer format, but come across poorly in a formal presentation?

2.1.1 Aristotle and Cicero—Rhetoric

Contemporary rhetoric (i.e., oral, not written, communication) attempts to affect the beliefs, attitudes, and actions of others. It melds principles of the great philosophers (e.g., Aristotle, Socrates, Plato, and Cicero) with modern psychology and digital advancements. To assess your current skill set, we need to determine your strengths and weaknesses.

First examine yourself within the context of Aristotle's three metrics: ethos, logos, and pathos. Reflect honestly on any comments you have received from professors, bosses, colleagues, and friends—positive or negative—that can provide objective insight on yourself. Given that smartphones and camcorders are ubiquitous these days, you have probably seen video and audio of yourself talking or interacting with others. Most likely, you have an impression or opinion about your voice or how your physical appearance (height, posture, etc.) comes across.

The table that follows takes you through an assessment of your strengths and weaknesses from Aristotle's perspective. Base the input you collect in this chapter on personal opinion, past experiences, outside feedback, and professional reviews. Fill out the tables with your "best guesses," then ask a friend or colleague to use the table to rank you. Rank each item using a scale of 1 to 10, with 10 being the highest.

Area of Analysis	Rating	Notes
ETHOS		
I am trusted as a person of good character.		
I am seen as a reliable professional.		
I am perceived as fair.		
LOGOS		
I communicate in a logical format. Any audience, regardless of its intelligence level, can follow my reasoning and arguments.		
I simplify information to meet each audience.		
I prioritize information and arguments.		
I am clear and concise.		
I offer creative resolutions and ideas to solve a problem.		
I think outside the box.		

Area of Analysis	Rating	Notes
PATHOS		
I project the right emotion, in the right dosage, for each situation.		
I portray credible emotion at the right time and intensity as appropriate.		
I remain calm in a heated moment.		
I can pick up on cues from the audience (perceptive). I sense what a person is thinking, feeling, or wanting based on body language and commentary.		
I identify issues raised in the audience or clients based on their reaction to my communication or advice.		

2.1.2 Personal Description

Next, let's find out who you are and who you want to become. If a colleague were to describe you and your work, what words would she choose to paint a picture of you? Through the years, I have heard many words to describe attorneys. I include them in the table below to help you describe yourself. Then think about how you would like to be perceived (ethos!). Reflect on how you want your legal career to take shape over the next five, ten, twenty years and how improving your oral presentation skills can help you achieve that goal. To create your ethos in the present, you need to have a direction for the future. Finally, think about attorneys you admire; what qualities do you see in those attorneys that you wish to emulate? Complete the table below and ask a colleague to do so as well.

Area of Analysis	Self-Assessment
What five words best describe you? *You can choose from the list below:* **Approachable** **Brilliant** **Capable** **Compelling** **Competent** **Concerned** **Confident** **Credible** **Dynamic** **Friendly** **Interesting** **Leader** **Memorable** **Natural** **Problem-Solver** **Relevant** **Reliable** **Subject Matter Expert** **Thoughtful**	1. 2. 3. 4. 5.

Area of Analysis	Self-Assessment
What five words best reflect how you would like to be described by clients and colleagues? *You can choose from the list below:* **Approachable** **Brilliant** **Capable** **Compelling** **Competent** **Concerned** **Confident** **Credible** **Dynamic** **Friendly** **Interesting** **Leader** **Memorable** **Natural** **Problem-Solver** **Relevant** **Reliable** **Subject Matter Expert** **Thoughtful**	1. 2. 3. 4. 5.
Where do you see your professional career in five, ten, twenty years?	
In your specific area of expertise, who do you admire and why?	
Who do you admire as a public speaker and why?	
Who do you admire as a leader and why?	

2.1.3 Scenario Rankings

It's time to do a gut check on where you think you stand on the different scenarios that demand oral communication that you will encounter in the legal profession. Review the following table of situations and corresponding elements of style, and note where you need work and where you think you already succeed. Again, ask a friend or colleague to complete this table with you, using a ranking scale of success between 1 and 10, with 10 being the highest.

	Substance (Clear Messaging)	Voice and Speech Pattern	Posture and Poise	Gestures	Emotion
Phone Calls					
One-on-one interactions with subordinate					
One-on-one interactions with colleague					
One-on-one interactions with superior					
One-on-one interactions with opposing counsel					
Interviews					
Existing client meetings					
Pitches					
Leading small group					
Impromptu presentations — small group					

	Substance (Clear Messaging)	Voice and Speech Pattern	Posture and Poise	Gestures	Emotion
Impromptu presentations — large group					
Formal presentations— small group					
Formal presentations— large group					

2.2   Big Picture of Improvement

You accomplish change by:

- setting goals;

- learning to write the spoken word;

- understanding and improving the techniques that enhance the elements of style in your presentations;

- rehearsing properly and incorporating the right elements of style into each presentation.

Just as if I met with you in a coaching session for a particular project, my system of helping you improve your oral communications skills will look like this:

Set Goals ⟹ Write ⟹ Rehearse ⟹ Perform

2.2.1 Set Goals

There are short-term and long-term goals. Use the assessments to establish your goals for improvement in each of the elements of style. As for your skill development, in which types of oral communication are you successful? In what areas do you know you need improvement? Regarding specific projects or presentations on which you might be working, who is the audience? What does the audience want and need to hear? What are your main themes? What is your purpose—to inform, educate, establish credibility, lead, or persuade?

I will help you learn how to set goals.

2.2.2 *Write*

We will work on crafting the oral communication so that it flows logically, simply, and in digestible sound bites. This requires you to focus on the main themes, creating impressions through stories, writing in points of relief, and using words and language that fit the audience instead of legal jargon. You will also learn to advantageously use literary tools to craft a memorable presentation. Your objective is to control the listener's impression with solid structure, flow, and emphasis.

Before we can fix stylistic components of oral communication (voice, body language, and emotion), we must have good material with which to work. Selecting and creating good substance (writing, messaging, and themes) provides the material you need to practice changing personal stylistic techniques. If you don't have good material available, complete the exercises in this book using selections from literature.

2.2.3 *Rehearse*

Rehearsing and practicing help calm the inevitable nerves associated with oral communication. However, as any golfer knows, rehearsing a bad swing only further impairs your game; moreover, you develop additional bad habits to compensate for an ingrained and poorly executed swing. Rehearsing in a manner that will improve your presentation requires you to tackle the elements of style in order:

- voice/speech pattern;

- body language;

- emotion.

2.2.3.1   Voice/Speech Pattern

The first area for improvement is voice and speech pattern.[1] Why? I believe the absence of proper voice education has damaged our profession. Poor communication skills contribute to:

1. *Relationship breakdown with colleagues, advisors, and audiences.* Email and written communication lend themselves to misinterpretation. Often, a brief phone call or face-to-face communication leaves no question

---

1. "Voice" refers to the sound quality of one's voice. "Speech pattern" refers to pacing, pauses, cadence, and inflection.

about the intention of the parties. Instead, attorneys rely on rapid-fire, abbreviated written communications, which leave parties questioning the meaning behind the messages. Eventually, relationships break down with each additional miscommunication.

2. *Increased glossophobia (the fear of public speaking).* Speaking in public can be frightening. Self-doubt and insecurities overpower reason and paralyze us. Deciding whether or not to use oral communication becomes a risk-reward analysis. Since most attorneys have not learned the skills necessary to successfully speak in public, they consider the risk too high. They don't want to take the risk of oral presentation. The risk is higher than not speaking, to be sure, but the reward is also greater. If you can demonstrate to yourself that you can speak well in public, you'll overcome the fear and create a virtuous cycle of confidence that will help you excel in public forums.

3. *A lack of capable leaders.* Think back to recent American presidents who have been great leaders—Reagan, Clinton. These men were at the top, not for what they wrote, but because of how they spoke to us. Some mocked their simplicity, but, as we have been saying, *simplicity* is a critical piece of communication. Many attorneys have the legal education and experience to have a successful career, but are not developing to their fullest leadership potential because they cannot communicate well. Audiences, including clients, look for a leader who can inspire, direct, and move us forward. We expect our leaders to be charismatic, and oral communication is a key component of charisma. We look for someone to follow, and few lawyers are *speaking up* effectively (pun intended).

4. *An entire generation of lawyers without proper command of their voice.* Attorneys use their voice to advise clients, to manage cases and deals, and to otherwise perform competently. Among the components of rhetoric, vocal and speech patterns also take the most time to correct, since we learn those habits from childhood. I begin working on the voice so you can start immediately with exercises for improvement.

2.2.3.2   Body Language

Body language includes poise, posture, gestures, and overall energy. I will help you incorporate visuals into your body language and alert you to some of the pitfalls I have seen. Nonverbal skills, such as listening, are also critical for improving an audience's impression of you.

2.2.3.3   Emotion

Emotion is one of the least talked about deficiencies that I have noticed in presentation skills. Getting it right requires training. Emotion encompasses everything from overall poise to executing the right emotion in any given circumstance. Properly using emotion takes initiative, effort, and self-awareness. Learning to act adds dynamics to round out the rehearsal process covered in this book. You can raise the overall level of your presentation skills, but *dynamics* help bring the variation that keeps an audience interested past the three- to five-minute mark. Proper rehearsal and preparation techniques keep a presentation fresh and help avoid robotic tendencies.

2.2.3.4   Implementation

These stylistic elements, which contribute to the success of the presentation, need to be implemented properly. You must practice out loud, and for optimal improvement, review a video or audio recording of you making or practicing a presentation. I will have you memorize the introduction and conclusion of every oral communication. You will avoid reading the main presentation word-for-word from the text, but instead practice until you can speak from bullet points or an outline. To make the presentation come to life with all the elements of style—including pace, pause, voice work, emotion, and gestures—you will need to practice. Through rehearsal, we will improve your voice, speech pattern, body language, emotion, and dynamics.

2.2.4 *Perform*

Eventually you will use effective presentation techniques. The goal is for you to 1) connect with the audience using eye contact; 2) employ good vocal technique and a clear speech pattern in any length of oral presentation; 3) express yourself properly and powerfully with body language that fits the situation and contains effective gestures, poise, and physical presence; and 4) use effective visuals that accentuate the messaging without distracting the audience. I will help you perform more effectively in your oral communications.

2.3   The Way Forward

In the chapters that follow, use the coaching exercises and ideas for your personal improvement. You've spent time in this chapter finding out where you currently stand, and it's time to move forward. Not every idea will help or resonate with you. You may wonder if the exercises will always take so much time. They won't. Eventually, practice changes habits and the new habit becomes a part of you. Eventually, you will reach a point when you do not need to take notes about how to write the presentation; you will just start writing it because you've trained your mind to organize thoughts for an oral presentation. Forming new habits takes time, repetition, and effort.

All the hard work, as Cicero knew, will pay off in the end. The teaching faculty at the National Institute for Trial Advocacy (NITA) has seen the fruit of hard work in oral communication training. James Brosnahan, a legend among NITA faculty, and I share a common mission to improve the oral communication skills of all attorneys:

> To me advocacy is somewhat similar to an athletic event, but in the need for training and spontaneity. Training: in terms of delivery, voice, building of suspense, mastering emotional presentations. Spontaneity: because, in the end, there are no steadfast rules, but only opportunities that need to be applied at the moment. We can never be quite sure what any witness will say or what Justice Scalia might [have asked]. That is why NITA is sponsoring this book.

And whether you argue before the Supreme Court, negotiate a credit agreement with a syndicate of banks, appear before a real estate zoning board, or serve as in-house counsel to a widget-maker, your oral communication skills can improve.

CHAPTER THREE

WRITE TO SPEAK

"Chance favors the prepared mind."

—*Louis Pasteur*

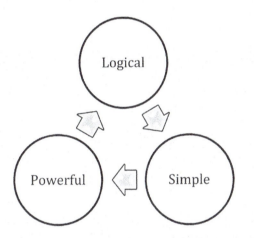

You have been trained to write as an attorney, which is appropriate given that your firm and your client expect excellent writing skills. However, to write text for oral presentation (anything from basic bullet point notes to full-blown Power-Point decks), you need to develop different skills to effectively communicate your message.

In an oral presentation, logical, simple, and powerful speech communicates most effectively. "Simple" is often difficult for attorneys who love long lists (i.e., those that follow "including, but not limited to . . ."), but you must sacrifice lengthy explanations, which are typical in written communication, in favor of simpler, more surgically spoken points. Remember, you have many more tools beyond the words you speak to convey your message in an oral presentation (e.g., vocal tone, emotion, eye contact, body language, cadence, etc., and sometimes a deck of slides). These extras enhance and complete the message.

3.1   Speak or Write?

Before you even begin thinking about what to say, decide if you should speak the message or write it. There are communications that you need evidenced. Others you need to use persuasive powers and avoid the confusion of an unclear tone. Your first decision should be whether to use written or oral communication. Otherwise, if you are like most lawyers, you will default to a lengthy written communication that the client might not understand or read (or could react to with hostility!). Ask yourself:

- What is my goal?

- Who is my audience? (Is the topic familiar, new, or controversial? Does the audience have a preexisting expectation or preference on how the information will be received? Do you know the audience? Does the audience know you?)

- What are my main themes?

- What is the best avenue of communication—written or spoken?

Here is an example. Pretend you represent a client who is the sole owner of a business that is in the process of being sold. You have a phone call scheduled in a few hours to review your mark-up of the stock purchase agreement.

- *What is my goal?* To highlight the major issues requiring input from the owner.

- *Who is the audience?* The owner, who is usually short on time and prefers a one-page recommendation that can be discussed on the phone.

- *What are my main themes?* Provide context for the issues, explain what is "market," lay out the owner's options, and explain your recommendation.

- *What is the best avenue of communication—written or spoken?* In this case, you need something written, which can be reviewed before a phone call, so the discussion can be productive.

Through this quick, one-minute exercise, you can identify the appropriate path forward, allowing you to provide the appropriate material before the call and use your time on the phone efficiently. Now you can begin the call with a goal and end it with an achievement. This kind of quick preparation will guide effective communication in advance of and during a call.

3.2 Priming Your Brain

Assume you have decided an oral communication is necessary. Let's explore the way to write for an oral presentation. When you speak, you connect with the listener by employing the principles of good rhetoric—ethos, pathos, logos, discipline, perceptiveness, and creativity—that Aristotle and Cicero taught. To craft a presentation that can showcase these elements, you must think critically.

Critical thinking consists of accurate analysis, reflection, and construction. Once you decide to speak, you analyze the problem, reflect on the relevant facts and problems, and decide how to construct your delivery of the message. You can train yourself to think about presentations by taking notes in an organized fashion before every call, conversation, or presentation until the preparation becomes a habit.

Contemporary rhetoric attempts to affect the beliefs, attitudes, and actions of the audience. It pulls together principles from Aristotle and Cicero with modern psychiatry, education, and technological advancements. This process of organizing your thoughts simplifies your message.

Your goal is to make thinking in a skeletal format a habit. There are several benefits of skeletal thinking:

1. *Speaking extemporaneously.* Too often, I meet attorneys who are comfortable with an oral communication only if they have been given ample time to prepare. Unfortunately, the practice of law requires many "on the spot" moments of genius. You can train to improve your skills with impromptu challenges.

2. *Delivering concise messages.* Attorneys, clients, assistants, and advisors are short on time. With an oral presentation, you will gain more ground by delivering the executive summary to an audience before diving into the details. This approach also increases the likelihood that you gain insight into what really matters to the audience. It's hard to discover what really matters to a client if you spend all your time speaking and little time listening.

3. *Explaining complicated matters in simple terms.* The best attorneys can describe complicated matters in a concise and simple message. Some people naturally acquire this skill; others must train their minds to narrow the issues and information into simple points. Think about tax attorneys. The ones who impress clients are those who can describe a difficult code provision with practical bottom-line application.

The following is an exercise to help begin this new mental training.

Skeletal Thinking Exercise

1. Before you leave the office, take a pen and sheet of paper and set a watch or timer for sixty seconds.

2. Recall a matter you handled during the day. Pick a fictitious audience to whom you will describe the matter—a client, managing partner, or new associate. Before the timer sounds, write three bullet points identifying the problem, describing the options, and providing a recommendation (analysis, reflection, and construction).

3. Go home, leaving the paper on your desk.

4. In the morning, before the day begins, record yourself orally presenting the matter in two to three minutes. Use only those bullet points.

5. Listen to the recording and think about ways to improve the clarity and simplicity of your communication.

6. As you become better, shrink the time to outline the presentation from sixty to thirty seconds.

7. Once you become faster at thinking in a skeletal, organized manner, increase the complexity of the matter and force yourself to simplify more complicated problems.

3.3   Meeting the Needs of Your Audience

Attorneys can glean many lessons from playwrights and screenwriters on the importance of understanding and defining an audience. Here are some guidelines for writing a presentation for an audience:

1. *Deliver in three-minute segments.* Audiences have short attention spans. Generally, an audience will listen for three minutes at a time. This timeframe stays fairly consistent over different levels of education and socio-economic status. Lincoln delivered the Gettysburg Address in approximately three minutes. To keep the attention of an audience, you need to "reset their clock" every three to four minutes by changing topics, posture, attitude, or voice. Edit your presentation so that it becomes a succession of three-minute windows. Each window represents a frame or time limit. At the end of the three-minute section, you need to shift the presentation in some way.

   One shift that playwrights and screenwriters use is emotional variation. Audiences need relief from staleness. Audiences require breaks from a singular emotion. Even in Shakespeare's most dramatic plays, he uses moments of comedy to break the heavy emotion and hit the audience's "reset button." Similarly, you need to change the emotion in a presentation. Tax attorneys need to portray enthusiasm when explaining a dull provision in the code or they run the risk of putting the audience to sleep.

Even a pro bono death penalty case requires appropriate emotional variation, because the appellate court cannot tolerate the consistent drip of depressing facts.

2. *Be sensitive to biases.* Every audience has biases. The audience members arrive at a presentation or jump on that phone call with a bag full of personal and professional biases. If possible, identify or anticipate these biases and address them. Ignoring them will keep you from connecting fully with the audience. Remember, Aristotle's logos, ethos, and pathos. How you use these tools will depend on how you perceive the audience's bias. Investigate the audience and address their perspectives and concerns. Sometimes, these biases impact a simple component of delivery (e.g., a New York litigator trying a case in southern Alabama may want to tone down his style to be more regionally in tune and palatable to the bench and jurors). Craft the content, elements of style, and delivery of the message in a way that will win the audience.

3. *Use primacy and recency.* Playwrights and screenwriters follow the rules of primacy and recency: audiences remember what they hear first and last. These principles were recognized in Greek dramas and are acknowledged in modern psychology. Put this into practice. The opening and closing must stand alone in excellence and meaning.

4. *Combine auditory and visual elements.* Audiences remember the most information when you send it through auditory and visual pathways. Visual components can be vivid facial or hand gestures, a flip chart, or a fancy PowerPoint. We can usually incorporate a visual component in a face-to-face meeting. Don't forget the visual pathway can be used on phone calls. Sending out a short outline of the call via email (remember the sixty-second exercise) will ensure everyone has a roadmap during the call and written reinforcement of your message after the conversation. The outline should, of course, complement your presentation.

5. *Be clear and concise.* Audiences want to learn. They want to understand what you are saying. They crave concise messages, and as few of them as possible. They do not tolerate long, meandering chatter that leads them down a rabbit hole.

6. *Use the vernacular.* Communicate with the language of the audience. When speaking to a board of directors, tailor your word choices to those words that are familiar to them. If you are talking to a doctor in a medical malpractice suit, use appropriate vocabulary (and, of course, understand the words you use).

After you write any presentation, think about a checklist that will ensure you have attended to the needs of your audience. This will speed editing future drafts, and eventually you should start writing your presentation with those needs in the forefront of your mind.

3.4   Theme-Crafting and Finding the Super-Objective

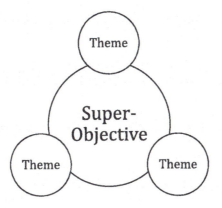

Once you simplify your message and attend to the needs of your audience, turn your attention to crafting an effective super-objective. A super-objective in acting is something the character wants for the entire play—a desire that underlies and explains everything the character does in the play—but is not necessarily known explicitly by the audience. After you identify and commit to a super-objective, develop themes to carry your presentation. By using minimal and clear themes, you help your audience better retain and comprehend the information. Excellent themes are built on a clear super-objective. There may be many main themes or points in a long presentation, but there is always one super-objective. When you clearly define a super-objective, you will create a clearer and more powerful performance. If you achieve your super-objective, what will be the immediate results?

Once you define and commit to a super-objective, you can begin choosing the appropriate theme(s). Sometimes you have one theme, but you can have several within a presentation. For example, at the end a client pitch, the client's needs and questions were addressed under the super-objective of "winning the mandate." During the pitch, you covered the themes of global representation and cost effectiveness.

Once you define your themes, you can collect supporting facts or statements that fit your themes. To keep the audience tuned to your themes, use headlining to highlight for the audience the takeaway or heading of the next section. These headlines should be forceful, brief, meaningful, and clear. Some themes become so clear that they morph into a refrain, like a song. Here, the theme is repeated word for word (hopefully with different stylistic delivery methods) to emphasize the theme throughout. Sometimes a clever theme has words with double meaning. John F. Kennedy's "Let Them Come to Berlin" speech is a perfect example. "Let them come to Berlin" has meaning on a level that is different than the simple words:

> There are many people in the world who really don't understand, or say they don't, what is the great issue between the free world and the Communist world. Let them come to Berlin.

There are some who say that Communism is the wave of the future. Let them come to Berlin.

And there are some who say in Europe and elsewhere we can work with the Communists. Let them come to Berlin.

And there are even a few who say that it is true that Communism is an evil system, but it permits us to make economic progress. *Lass'sienach Berlin kommen*. Let them come to Berlin."

Once you commit to a super-objective, pick your themes, and pad them with supporting facts and arguments. The table below demonstrates the structural organization for outlining a presentation.

Structural Organization

Super-objective: if your presentation is a success, what do you want to be the immediate result or impact?

Main Themes: what must the audience understand and remember from your presentation?

1. Headline your theme

Supporting facts/arguments:

2. Headline your theme

Supporting facts/arguments:

3. Headline your theme

Supporting facts/arguments:

Each major section of a presentation should have a theme or main point and should be able to stand alone.

Having strong, clear themes that can operate independently, if needed, helps when you are asked questions. You can immediately recall a section relevant to the question, answer it intelligently, and return to the place you left off in the presentation. Some audiences ask questions that precede where you are in the presentation (the answer is coming). Other questions emerge that indicate the audience member misunderstands a previously covered point. Having themes helps you answer a question and dive back into the presentation at a logical place.

Crafting strong themes means you make choices. Out of the endless possible directions, you triage information and pick the few themes that will give you the strongest chance of connecting and convincing the audience. Remember the motto "sometimes, less is more" and keep your communications structured, simple, and focused.

3.5 Picking a Format for Delivery

The format you pick for any delivery—no matter how short or long, casual or formal—gives the audience an immediate insight into your purpose and scope. Reflect this format in the outline of the presentation. The audience will feel at ease knowing where you will lead them. It gives them an immediate roadmap. You can make each oral communication presentation more powerful and directed by making a thoughtful choice on the verb voice and tense used. You may decide to lead a call, describing things with "we," the first-person plural verb form, to subliminally gain agreement. Using the past tense can also confirm the buy-in of the audience to an issue that wasn't expressly agreed on. Some presentations demand a certain format, but I encourage you to pick a format that most audiences naturally recognize:

- *General to particular.* This is an excellent path with an unsophisticated audience. Start at a high-level, introduce essential principles, and then get into the details. The key is to win the audience with the essential principles.

- *Particular to general.* You are trying to help the audience see the forest through the trees. You take them from the details to a 10,000-foot view of the problem.

- *Enumeration.* Here, you have a definite number of precise points that are made in order—"1, 2, 3"— but be sure to keep the number of points between three and five. No one can remember more than that.

- *Sensory (story telling).*[1] Many of us learn best through stories; whether in books at bedtime, family tales, fables, literature, and history, stories help us connect. A good story has a clear beginning, middle, and end; it sets up a problem and offers a solution. A well-chosen story can help make a direct or subtle appeal to morality or justice in a way that nails the point and is remembered without being preachy or overbearing.

- *Chronological.* Don't assume this is a boring method to choose. We frame our lives by clocks and calendars and what happened at a particular time and date. The only way that flashbacks and parallel dating becomes a successful method is because the orator commits to tell the facts with time as the foundation. Clients universally want to find out "what comes next," and, if appropriate, a presentation laying out a chronological path forward can be very compelling. This method should be familiar to every attorney.

- *Compare/Contrast.* I see great success with this format when you are helping a client see the positives and negatives about a certain decision. Simple columns with pros and cons help organize a compare and contrast system. You can add decision trees and visuals easily to this method. This style also provides an attorney the ability to let the client make a well-informed strategic choice knowing the range of consequences that spring from a particular decision.

---

1. *See* "Pre-packs" section below in this chapter for advice on how to prepare stories, analogies, or hypotheticals.

3.6   Opening and Shutting Your Mouth

Beginning/Opening

Grabs attention

Establishes credibility /
authority on the subject

Puts forth a strong theme—the foundation
to achieve the super objective

Ending/Closing

Summarizes a strong theme

Demands something of the audience

Ends gracefully

If you only have an hour to prepare an oral communication, spend fifty-nine minutes on the opening and closing. Decide what to say when you open and shut your mouth, memorize the text, and you'll set yourself up for success. Openings and closings need good structure and solid rehearsal. A successful opening must:

- grab attention;
- establish credibility/authority on the subject; and
- put forth a strong theme.

A solid closing:

- summarizes a strong theme;

- demands something of the audience (e.g., "Please consider this information and let me know how you want to proceed"; or "Your Honor, we ask for summary judgment."); and

- gracefully ends.

3.7 Preparing for Different Audiences

You face a wide range of presentations as an attorney, each of which requires excellent written preparation. Here are many of the scenarios that you encounter, of which you already performed a stylistic self-assessment in the previous chapter:

- telephone calls;

- one-on-one interactions with subordinates;

- one-on-one interactions with superiors;

- one-on-one interactions with adversaries;

- one-on-one interactions with colleagues;

- one-on-one interactions with client advisors;

- one-on-one interactions with co-counsel;

- interviews;

- client meetings;

- leading teams;

- impromptu presentations—small group;

- impromptu presentations—large group;

- formal presentations—small group; and

- formal presentations—large group.

You need to develop your writing strengths for each of these scenarios. Most attorneys will encounter an oral communication opportunity in each situation. Begin to find patterns in your practice. Notice situations that you frequently encounter and make certain you are well-prepared using the writing tips in this chapter.

As you proceed through this book, practice different skills of style (voice, speech pattern, gestures, emotion) by pretending to present to each of these audiences. You may discover that your interview experience is lacking, but your skill for writing a presentation for a small group is well developed. Once you identify your weaknesses, continue to practice writing for those audiences until you gain momentum, speed, and strength in those areas. When you practice in an artificial scenario, why not push yourself towards the harder personal challenge?

3.8   Preparing the Self-Branding

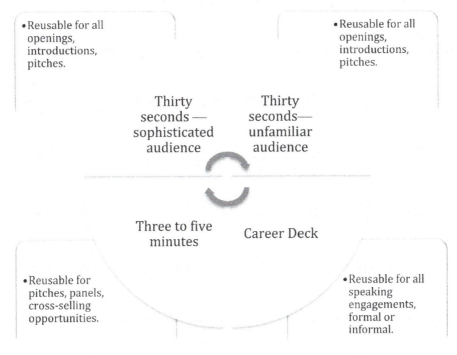

In your toolbox, you must have presentations that are well-written, practiced, and memorized. These will be used over and over, allowing you to prepare for presentations efficiently by using great material that is ready to showcase. These include:

- thirty-second description of yourself for an audience sophisticated with your legal specialty;

- thirty-second description of yourself for an audience unfamiliar with your legal specialty;

- three- to five-minute description of yourself with specific examples of success; and

- formal pitch deck describing major milestones/matters/cases in your legal career with appropriate graphics.

These four presentations, if properly done, will become a lifeline for every communication you encounter. The thirty-second self-description/introduction easily morphs into any opening for a presentation or any introduction you need to make in a social setting. The three- to five-minute description can become your contribution to a group pitch or the dialogue that follows a casual meeting with a prospective client. The formal pitch deck becomes a resource that you use over and over again when called on to give presentations. Write the presentation in three-minute chunks and practice each new section; moving forward, you won't have to reinvent the wheel every time you are asked to talk about a matter or relate a previous case to a current problem.

The self-branding material every attorney should have prepared and practiced is outlined in the table below.

| Thirty seconds, sophisticated audience | • Practice area
• Years in practice
• Niche within firm/government
• Firm and its branding message |

| Thirty seconds, unfamiliar audience | • Education
• Layman description of legal work
• Example of practical application
• Discussion of firm/government position |

| Three to five minutes | • One to two minutes about the firm and its areas of expertise
• Two to three minutes about your specific area of expertise
• Examples |

| Career deck | • Three minute Education section
• Three minute Career history section
• Three minute peronal interests
• Three minute on each major milestone/matter/case in career |

First write your thirty-second presentations word-for-word. Writing about yourself—your legal practice and experience—takes careful wordsmithing. It will help to practice the text with trusted friends or colleagues, giving you a chance to explore the best word choices. When Aristotle talked about ethos (manifesting good character), he had the data points for public speakers at his fingertips. Aristotle moved in small circles within Greece's aristocracy, and he and the populace at large knew the reputation of the speaker. Today, you have your opening remarks to establish ethos. You walk a fine line of establishing credibility without being perceived as conceited. You need to gain the audience's respect in a short time frame, so practice makes perfect.

Below is a group exercise to practice your openings and self-branding material. Find a few colleagues to meet and deliver personal descriptions. Bounce ideas off each other to find the best word choices to describe your experience and expertise.

Word Choice Group Exercise

Present a thirty- to sixty-second personal description to a small group and brainstorm with them about improvements in phrasing and/or word choice.

Presenter	Strength of word choice when describing self	Creative firm or practice descriptions	Successes and improvement recommendations

Once you feel confident that you have chosen simple, clear, and strong words to describe yourself, begin changing your longhand text into simple bullet points. These bullet points will become your launching pad for memorizing the messages. Memorizing your opening is essential to convince the audience of your confidence and intelligence. I am always shocked at the number of attorneys who read a description of themselves and their practice from a piece of paper, down to their name and their firm's name.

3.9   Preparing the Impromptu

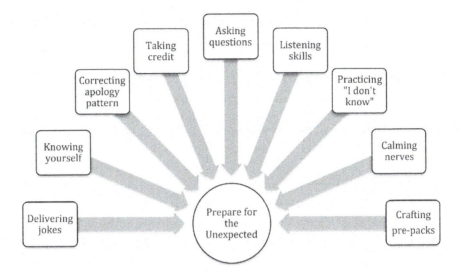

Many oral communications cannot be planned. Even a planned presentation will go wrong. Every presentation you deliver will be riddled with mistakes. You can't prepare for every interruption or question in a meeting or on a phone call. Unanticipated questions are asked of you, and you must have intelligent responses. In addition, you'll encounter oral communication opportunities that are completely unscripted and unplanned. There are tricks to help you with impromptu encounters.

3.9.1 Delivering Jokes

Knowing how to help an audience feel welcome and at ease is essential for any good orator. If you are not naturally funny, you can practice jokes and ways to make your audience feel relaxed. I know attorneys who keep a log of interesting statistics, funny stories, history, and classic jokes. I refer to classic jokes as comedy appropriate for any audience age and disposition. Racial, sexual, and edgy comedy is rarely well received by an audience—and not worth the risk. Stick with "G-rated" material and intelligent play on words, especially those that fix the audience, subject matter, or occasion.

3.9.2 Knowing Yourself

Realize whether you generally answer a question directly or indirectly. Understand if and when you show obvious nerves when you respond to a certain person in your workplace who puts you on edge.

3.9.3 Correcting Apology Pattern

Apology patterns often follow two extremes down gender lines. Women generally apologize for too much, and men generally don't apologize when they should.[2] Don't apologize for things outside your control. If you cause a problem, own up to it immediately. You would be surprised how confident this makes you look.

3.9.4 Taking Credit

The art of taking credit for work also swings on a pendulum with genders at either side. Women sometimes fail to take credit for work, ideas, or contributions within the business world; men are quicker to take credit for work, ideas, or contributions they did not author.[3]

3.9.5 Asking Questions

Know when and how to ask questions. Have you served on a board and realized that the verbose board member asks questions to hear his own voice? It's a common and distracting habit. Not only is it annoying, it impedes progress. Reflect on whether you ask insightful, relevant questions that either help clarify a confusing point or guide the discussion in your direction.

3.9.6 Listening Skills

Sometimes we fail in an unplanned communication because we fail to listen to the question. When an audience sees it is being ignored, the audience will respond in kind and shut down. You need to stay in the present moment, avoid thinking about your grocery list, and listen to the concerns of the audience.

3.9.7 Practicing "I Don't Know"

Through the course of a legal practice, it takes finesse to simultaneously admit that you do not know the answer to a question and maintain the confidence of a colleague or a client. I coach all my clients to create a practice-relevant list of ten "I don't know" answers, so they can respond intelligently and confidently to a question posed to them. Instead of stuttering and rambling, try a simple "I don't

---

2. Tannen, Deborah, "The Power of Talk: Who Gets Heard and Why." Harvard Business Review: HBR On Point 9977, 139–148 (1992).

3. AMERICAN POLITICAL SCIENCE REVIEW, August 2012, at 533–547; DOI: http://dx.doi.org/10.1017/S0003055412000329.

know" response that assures the audience that you will promptly find and deliver the answer. "I don't know, but I will call you back in an hour with an answer."

3.9.8 Calming Nerves[4]

Many people are shocked when they encounter an unrehearsed oral communication. Learning how to control the adrenaline is key to keeping a clear head. Try a few of these simple exercises to help manage those stress hormones:

- Put yourself in low-cost impromptu situations as frequently as possible. If you can regularize these encounters in your mind, you won't have a "deer in the headlights" reaction.

- Breathe. It's clichéd, but it works. Breathing helps diffuse those hormones and relieve the psychosomatic reaction. Breathe deeply and regularly. Often times, stress makes our breath shallow and irregular.

- Practice with friends. Ask colleagues or spouses or friends to spring questions on you.

- Record yourself in prime form. Record a prepared presentation that you enjoy giving and looks impressive. Review this presentation again and again until you can identify the things that make you proud of the style and substance. Your memory will help you mimic these winning qualities the next time an unplanned call springs up or question is asked.

3.9.9 Crafting "Pre-Packs"

By the time you are a third- or fourth-year associate, in-house counsel, or government attorney, you settle into certain specialties. As you begin to deepen and narrow your expertise, recurring scenarios arise with clients, colleagues, the bench, and industry specialists in your field. If you start to track the types and frequencies of questions or moments of confusion from your audiences, you will notice that most lawyers need ten to fifteen stock answers to field those repetitive questions. A great way to connect with the audience, be memorable, and communicate clearly is to weave pre-practiced responses. Craft ten to fifteen "pre-packs" to answer audience questions.

After collecting the list of recurring questions, set aside time to write effective pre-packs that include a hypothetical or story. Craft the stories that can reach a broad audience and can be adapted to various situations. A good pre-pack should take a couple of minutes to deliver and should give the audience a memorable picture of your message. Memorize the hypotheticals, and alter them as needed over time to meet changes in the law or your industry.

Use pre-packs as an excellent teaching tool for younger attorneys, when cross-selling within your firm, or to explain things to a client. Hypotheticals, which are

---

4. *See* Relaxation Exercise by personal trainer, Michelle Blake, in chapter four.

analogous stories, help you communicate well. A tax attorney explaining corporate tax rates can invent a perfect hypothetical to explain the global economic implications of changes in a country's corporate tax rate. A contract attorney can help a young associate understand performance obligations by giving an everyday contractual example using his son's lawn service.

Pre-Pack Exercise/Example

1. Look below at the definition of EBITDA taken from a standard credit agreement. Don't waste your time reading it. You can look at it and know that it's complex and wordy. Clearly, this definition should be read, not spoken, as it is a comprehensive provision in a broader credit agreement. For this exercise, pretend you have three minutes to explain this provision to a client or a judge. Pretend the client or judge just asked you: "Remind me, what does EBITDA mean?" In your response, you can use a pre-pack—a recycled, practiced explanation of a general understanding of EBITDA. If you practice corporate law or corporate litigation, this is a predictable, recurring explanation you need to have on hand for the noncognescenti.

   "Consolidated EBITDA" means for any period the sum of (i) Consolidated Net Income for such period (excluding therefrom (x) any extraordinary, unusual or non-recurring items of gain or loss, (y) any gain or loss from discontinued operations and (z) any gain or loss attributable to Asset Dispositions made other than in the ordinary course of business), plus (ii) to the extent not otherwise included in the determination of Consolidated Net Income for such period, all proceeds of business interruption insurance policies, if any, received during such period plus (iii) (without duplication) an amount which, in the determination of Consolidated Net Income for such period, has been deducted for (A) Consolidated Interest Expense, (B) provisions for Federal, state, local and foreign income, franchise, state single business unitary and similar taxes, (C) depreciation, amortization (including, without limitation, amortization of goodwill and other intangible assets), impairment of goodwill and other noncash charges or expenses (excluding any such noncash charge to the extent that it represents amortization of a prepaid cash expense that

---

was paid in a prior period), (D) noncash compensation expense, or other noncash expenses or charges, arising from the sale of stock, the granting of stock options, the granting of stock appreciation rights and similar arrangements (including any re-pricing, amendment, modification, substitution or change of any such stock, stock option, stock appreciation rights or similar arrangements), (E) noncash rent expense, (F) any financial advisory fees, accounting fees, legal fees and other similar advisory and consulting fees and related out-of-pocket expenses of the Borrower incurred as a result of the Transaction, all determined in accordance with GAAP, (G) Transaction related expenditures (including cash charges in respect of strategic market reviews, management bonuses or early retirement of Debt) described on Schedule 1.01B, (H) expenses incurred by Holdings or any Consolidated Subsidiary to the extent reimbursed in cash by a third party other than Holdings or one or more of its Consolidated Subsidiaries, (I) fees and expenses in connection with the satisfaction and discharge of the Senior Subordinated Notes, (J) unrealized losses on Derivatives Agreements, (K) losses from foreign currency adjustments, (L) losses in respect of pension or other post-retirement benefits or pension assets, (M) write-offs of deferred financing costs, (N) expenses in respect of earn-out obligations, (O) any financial advisory fees, accounting fees, legal fees and similar advisory and consulting fees and related out-of-pocket expenses of the Borrower and its Consolidated Subsidiaries incurred as a result of Permitted Business Acquisitions and/or Foreign Asset Dispositions and (P) cash charges and expenses in connections with employee or management relocation or severance costs, including, without limitation, related to Permitted Business Acquisitions and Dispositions, all determined in accordance with GAAP and in each case eliminating any increase or decrease in income resulting from noncash accounting adjustments made in connection with the related Permitted Business Acquisition or Foreign Asset Disposition, minus (iv) any amount which, in the determination of Consolidated Net Income for such period, has been added for any noncash income or noncash gains, all as determined in accordance with GAAP minus (v) the aggregate amount of cash payments made during such period in respect of any noncash accrual, reserve or other noncash charge or expense accounted for in a prior period and not otherwise reducing Consolidated Net Income for such period minus (vi) any amount which, in the determination of Consolidated Net Income for such period, has been added for interest income, unrealized gains on Derivatives Agreements, gains from foreign currency adjustments and gains in respect of pension or other post-retirement benefits or pension assets.

2. To write an effective pre-pack, set your super-objective, which in this case will be to explain EBITDA quickly and clearly. Next, identify your audience. For the first explanation, let's imagine a client or judge with little or no financial background.

3. Write a full explanation word-for-word, focusing on simplicity and clarity:

    EBITDA (earnings, before interest, tax, depreciation, and amortization) is generally used to measure the cash flow and general health of a business. Revenue is too general and does not give you a good picture of the health of a business. Net Income is too specific and may be burdened by too many details, *muddying* the waters. EBITDA yields a balanced view. Here is the calculation: Revenue minus the burden of the Direct Costs (e.g., the costs of goods sold) spent to create that revenue yields the Gross Profit; further burdening the Gross Profit by the indirect costs (i.e., the operating expenses, or all the day-to-day expenses, such as salaries, rent, marketing, and healthcare) yields the operating income (i.e., EBIT). Finally, you add back noncash expenses such as depreciation and amortization, to yield EBITDA—a snapshot of a company's cash flow and general health.

4. Edit some of the detail, leaving a more simple explanation. Save the detail for any follow-up questions that might arise.

    EBITDA (earnings, before interest, tax, depreciation, and amortization) is generally used to measure the cash flow and general health of a business. Revenue is too general and does not give you a good picture of the health of a business. Net Income is too specific and may be burdened by too many details, *muddying* the waters. EBITDA yields a balanced view.

5. Add an example to the edited answer, to be used if necessary.

    Example: Sally owns a mechanic shop, which grossed $1 million in revenue. After she pays for the company's direct costs (in this case, wages) of $500K and operating expenses—healthcare, rent, marketing, the depreciation on the equipment, etc., of $300K, she is left with operating income or EBIT of $200K. Adding back the $25K of noncash expenses (like depreciation) tells you how much cash Sally has left over—$225K is the EBITDA of Sally's company.

6. Narrow the fully written explanation into bullet points:

    -   EBITDA = earnings, before interest, tax, depreciation, and amortization.

    -   Operating income = everything left over after the company pays for salaries, rent, marketing, and healthcare.

    -   Adjustments for noncash expenses.

    -   Market uses EBITDA to judge the health of a company.

    -   Sally example.

7. Now change your audience to a more financially knowledgeable client or judge. Craft another pre-pack with more detail:

    EBITDA (earnings, before interest, tax, depreciation, and amortization) is a market standard metric used to measure the cash flow and general health of a business.

    Financial analysts do not measure the health of a business by simply looking at the *top line* (i.e., revenue is the top line of an income statement), because revenue is too high-level and does not provide insight into the cost structure of a business. For example, I may sell one million dollars' worth of chairs, but if my cost basis was also one million dollars (i.e., I bought the chairs for the same price that I sold them), I didn't make any money. Again, revenue only tells part of the story.

    Conversely, financial analysts do not measure the health of business by looking at the net income (i.e., the bottom line), either. This number is often burdened with too many expenses (including noncash expenses like depreciation), muddying the perspective on whether a company is healthy. For example, a company may have a lot of noncash expenses such as depreciation, which make it appear like the company didn't make money, when in fact it did.

EBITDA yields a balanced view (i.e., it is not unburdened by costs, but also not too heavily burdened by noncash costs) and is calculated as follows:

Revenue minus the direct costs ("costs of goods sold" or "COGS") related to that revenue yields the gross profit ("GP"). You can't stop at GP, because it ignores all the indirect costs (i.e., the day-to-day operating expenses—"Opex"—such as salaries, rent, marketing, and healthcare) the company incurs to operate. Assuming no depreciation expense is reflected in your COGS or Opex, then GP – (minus) Opex yields the operating income, which is also known as earnings before interest, tax, depreciation, and amortization ("EBITDA"). After that, you subtract depreciation and amortization, taxes, and interest, to arrive at Net Income. Unlike Net Income, EBITDA gives you a snapshot of a company's cash flow and general health without the confusing impact associated with noncash expenses, taxes, and interest.

Example: Sally owns a furniture store and managed to sell $1 million in chairs in one year. The chairs cost her a total of $600K; the cost to operate her business was $250K; therefore, EBITDA is $150K. She has noncash expenses of $150K, yielding a Net Income of $0.

Revenue $1 million

(–) COGS $600K

= GP $400K

(–) Opex $250K

= EBITDA $150K

(–) Depreciation $150K

= EBIT $0

(–) Taxes $0

= Net Income $0

Again, EBITDA is the common measure of a company's free cash flow and overall health.

8. Narrow the fully written explanation into bullet points, which end up being almost identical to the more simple pre-pack above. You can expand or contract the detail depending on the sophistication of your audience.

- EBITDA = earnings, before interest, tax, depreciation, and amortization.

- Operating income = everything left over after the company pays for salaries, rent, marketing, and healthcare.

- Adjustments for noncash expenses.

- Market uses EBITDA to judge the health of a company.

If your pre-packs are well written, you will recycle and adapt them. Keep them in your toolbox so you are prepared when the expected question or situation arises.

3.10 Additional Considerations

3.10.1 Gender Differences

At the beginning of the book, I told you to find your most successful substance and style without sacrificing your individuality. Your gender defines you in many ways and impacts your oral communications. I encourage both men and women to capitalize on those characteristics that make them male or female. If not overdone, doing so will enhance your performance. There are certainly dominant characteristics typical of each gender: males will more likely be accused of being statuesque or wimpy, while women will more likely be accused of being strident, melodramatic, or little. This book will not shy away from pointing out those differences for you when it comes to stylistic elements (voice, gestures, and emotion). Your writing should appeal equally to both genders.

See Chapter Ten, "Communication Issues for Women," for a discussion of the challenges women face in professional communication and tips for overcoming them.

3.10.2 Graphics

As a general rule, graphics and visuals should not distract attention from you. They should help the audience remember your points, follow the roadmap you provide, and increase their comprehension. Before you venture into the world of graphics, reach out to IT. If you don't have IT support, learn how to create simple graphics for printed handouts and for presentations. Your IT department will be able to show you quickly what style your firm (or governmental department) uses and what resources you have available to you. This saves time later.

I generally find attorneys over a certain age need help with graphics or visual aids that they need to control. If you cannot fix the technical problems in a presentation, arrange for someone to be there to provide assistance; alternatively, choose a medium you can handle. I always expect technology will fail, which forces me to practice the presentation without visuals. If you have essential visuals, print them out for audience members to have in case your multimedia equipment or software fails.

When the technology fails, never attempt to fix it on the spot unless it will take less than two minutes. Otherwise, ask someone to bring in help from the IT department and press forward. The audience is there to hear *you*—the graphics should be a backdrop.

3.10.3 Logistics

On a closing note, don't let the logistics of a presentation stop your success or cause stress. If you have an assistant, train and then rely on that assistant to help you stay organized. Set up a simple chart to stay organized. Like it or not, we live in a digital-savvy world that expects dazzling visuals. You need to develop a working knowledge of the software programs used to create presentations and graphics (e.g., Microsoft PowerPoint, Apple's Keynote, etc.). If you doubt your ability or time-strapped schedule, invest in someone's help to create simple graphics that can readily be used in your practice. Everyone can use a good timeline, a simple pie chart, a trending graph, and a comparison table.

	General Information	**Delegated Duties**
Event		
Date		
Participants		
Location		
Coordinator/contact info		
Handouts		
Equipment needs		
Time expectations		
Q&A preparation		
Room set up		
Other		

Chapter Four

Voice/Speech Basics—
Posture, Breath, Sound, and Quality

"The human voice is the organ of the soul."

—*Henry Wadsworth Longfellow*

In this chapter, some of the terms might be new to you. *Tone* refers to the quality of your voice, and it is often used to describe the overall message or emotion the voice emits. *Range* means the span of notes and pitches you use when speaking. *Resonance* refers to the vibrations of sound through all the chambers in your body that serve as speakers to amplify sound. *Upward inflection* is the upward tick in pitch, properly used at the end of questions or to keep attention in the midst of a series.

As we shift from *crafting the substance of a presentation* to *the elements of style*, keep in mind that some people naturally perform better than others. Some singers and orators have the gift of a great voice. Some professionals put you at ease or inspire you simply with their body language. If you are one of these individuals, you can become even more successful by training and developing your gift. If you are not naturally gifted, you can learn techniques that improve your skills.

Your goals are to:

- identify and ditch bad habits;
- cultivate good habits so you can employ them at their peak level; and
- enhance those good habits at which you already excel.

I encourage you to "practice in the extreme"—meaning, rehearse pieces and try exercises with more energy and exaggeration than you would in a presentation. Don't worry—when you present before an audience, your nerves will tame the practiced exaggeration. It is easier to pull back from an exaggerated performance than to push up from dull to enthusiastic.

4.1 What Type of Progress Can You Expect?

Improving your voice takes time, effort, and humility. Since improvements involve physical awareness and muscular development, they take time. Creating new habits requires repetition and hard work. Improving your voice is deeply personal, and requires you to check your ego at the door. You must breach these roadblocks to improving your voice if you are to improve, and this takes nerve. The hold of glossophobia is powerful. Ever wonder why a peer could be overcome with fright when asked to speak publically? Fear is often more difficult to overcome than pain. Each of us needs fortitude in small (or large) doses to confidently stand up in front of any audience and present or lead a meeting. So toughen up and prepare to enter a zone that is uncomfortable and often challenging—even for an experienced attorney.

Following the exercises in this book will improve your posture, breathing, sound, and vocal quality. Those included in this chapter are useful for attorneys and suitable for self-study. One way to achieve better results is to use video and audio recordings of your performances. Many attorneys fear being recorded—however, doing so provides you with an unbiased tool you can use to critique your presentation or exercise. I recently heard a voice instructor discussing the need for students to prove to themselves their need to learn before acquiring a new skill. There is nothing like a video review to show you what needs to be improved.

The table below is a progress plan for improving your voice. Some improvements can be made now and put into practice. Others require retraining muscles and will take time and practice to implement. Speech pathologists say it takes three to nine months to change the tone of one's voice. Be patient with your progress. Improving your voice is a lifelong endeavor because you will constantly find new things to improve.

If you have a recurring vocal issue that you or someone else identifies (e.g. gravelly or nasal voice), consider seeking medical advice before beginning any voice exercises. You may have an illness or anatomical barrier that these exercises cannot overcome. I have met attorneys with deviated septums, nodes on their vocal cords, and asthma. Until eliminated, the impediment prevented improvement. In addition, some vocal conditions, like stuttering, a heavy regional accent, or the inability to pronounce particular sounds, usually require a speech therapist. Remember to check with your doctor before beginning any new physical activity. And with the breath work, don't pass out!

Short-Term Goals	Long-Term Goals
Posture—Alignment	Posture—Core strength
Breath—Nerve control	Breath—Diaphragm
Sound—Volume	Breath—Regulation
Sound—Articulation	Sound—Resonance
Quality—Range	Quality—Pitch
Quality—Speed	Quality—Inflection
	Quality—Pauses

4.2   How the Voice Works

The human voice is an instrument. However, unlike many musical instruments, we cannot easily see the inner workings. Understanding its mechanics will help you improve your vocal quality. The goal is for you to speak effortlessly, with a strong, clear voice that projects pleasant and professional qualities—a voice that an audience will enjoy hearing.

Speech development begins in utero. A growing baby hears sounds and voices before birth. Once born, we cry to signal a need. Soon, we expand to gurgling and then phonetic sound. Sounds are joined in what may appear to be a game of repetition until speech is developed. Eventually, speech patterns are created, replete with regional language, accent, and tone quality.

Your voice has been influenced by the environment since before birth. Changing your voice or speech pattern takes time and care. Stylistic improvements sometimes take the longest. Remember that your voice defines you to any audience and can make or break a presentation. At times in your legal practice, your voice is the only stylistic tool to transmit your message . . . the all-important telephone call.

When you open your mouth to speak, the motor cortex of the brain sends a message to the lungs to intake air and expel it through the trachea. When the rush of air hits your voice box (larynx), the mucus membranes vibrate to produce sound. These membranes vibrate and create sound waves supported by airflow. Next, the waves of air pass through your throat and mouth. These chambers, along with the bony areas of your face and head, with movements of your lips, tongue, and teeth (articulators), enhance the timbre and intensity of your voice. This is resonance. We recognize it in the sounds of singers and musical instruments. Regulating the amount of air passing through the voice box, the rate of vibration within your vocal cords, and the parallel vibrations in your mouth, face, and head (to create resonance) affect the sound of your voice. Picture the human voice as a blend of a horn and string instrument. The horn component is the focused air that gives voice to a trumpet. The string components are the vibrating vocal cords and the vibrations within our resonators.

Air fuels the voice. It regulates the quality and the volume of the voice. You must fill your lungs completely and release air gradually to produce a full, audible sound. The support for this breath is our skeletal posture. If you want to improve your voice, you must start by improving your posture and then add proper breathing techniques.

You may have heard that great speakers and singers breathe using their diaphragm. They maximize their breath by exercising the intercostal muscles that cradle the ribs to broaden their breath. To lengthen their breath, they use their diaphragms (actually, it's the muscles surrounding the diaphragm that you control) by opening up torso space. Good posture—shoulders back, rib cage lifted, and a relaxed abdominal area—is an element of this process. Proper alignment and core abdomen muscles support create the foundation your voice needs to work at its optimal level. Once you achieve good posture, you can improve your breathing, and ultimately, your voice. I address this more later, but for now remember your mom's scolding: "stand tall" and "sit up."

You support effective breathing with your intercostal muscles and diaphragm. The diaphragm expands when you inhale, and contracts so you can exhale. Using your diaphragm and surrounding muscle groups to control breathing also helps you calm your nerves. A calming breath taken in through your nose can help relieve jitters, allowing your mind to focus before and during a presentation. Finally, you must be able to control your exhalation so you can properly regulate sound and volume.

The muscles in your throat, face, mouth, and tongue control the tone or quality of your voice. Tightly constricted muscles in these areas create a thin, tense sound. One way to relax and stay un-constricted is to yawn with your mouth closed. I've witnessed good orators doing this to ease their nerves before a presentation. Yawning stretches the back of the throat and gently reminds the throat and mouth muscles to work effortlessly. Give it a try.

Relaxing your throat through that closed yawn will also convince you that you can perceive and control many variables of your voice—tension, high and low registers, volume variation, and overall vocal quality. As you expand your voice, you will expand your ability to express yourself more fully in different situations.

4.3 Components of Voice and Speech and How Your Voice Affects a Listener

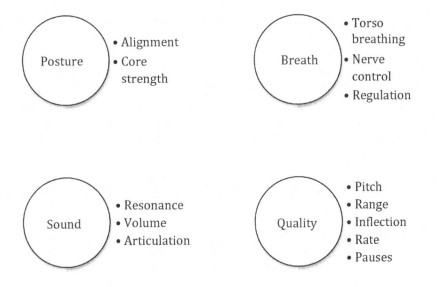

The quality of a voice reveals a vast amount about the speaker. Think of your first impression when talking with a person on the phone. The only sense affected in a phone call is your hearing. Listening blindly to a voice reveals education, attitude, emotion, age, personality, and gender. Since so much of your work as an attorney is done on the phone, think about how much more persuasive you could be if you improved the quality of your voice.

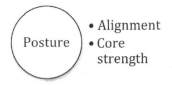

Experts in body language confirm that before a speaker even opens his mouth, an audience assesses him based on his posture. Many first and last impressions are shaped by posture. It is also the first building block to a powerful voice.

An audience notices your physical alignment when you are both standing and seated. Most of you spend the workday seated, and a bad alignment habit may already have taken hold. Master sitting first. As you progress in your career and prestige, you may stand more often before an audience. Learning to sit and stand properly will help build your confidence and help you take command of the room. Proper alignment reflects confidence and puts your body in the optimal position to make you feel confident. In short, you assume an athletic posture—not exaggerated—which generally readies your body to move easily when necessary or appropriate.

When correcting posture problems, men generally overcorrect by shifting to a rigid stance that looks stiff and unapproachable. Women generally must expand beyond what is naturally comfortable to avoid looking small and minimized. Because women generally have a smaller size and frame than men, bad posture is more noticeable. It is almost impossible for female attorneys to compete visually in a room full of men without good posture.

Good posture takes endurance and strength. Regular exercise helps you maintain good posture. For both men and women, good alignment also helps with overall energy. You build muscles that power your voice. Speaking is hard work. Maintaining good alignment for hours on end is exhausting without strength and endurance. In addition, audiences can detect muscle weakness. The same muscles used in good posture provide strength for breathing and make you appear more confident.

As attorneys, we must improve posture both seated and standing. Litigators and transactional attorneys must equally display powerful posture while standing and sitting. Practice each exercise listed below regularly. The goal of these exercises is to correct a slumped and weak-looking stance, create an image of command and confidence, and open and strengthen the muscles that support breathing.

4.3.1 Alignment

Alignment Exercise—Standing

1. Stand up.

2. Roll your head gently from one shoulder to the other and back again.

3. While looking at the floor, stretch your arms high into the air, grasping with your fingertips at the highest point possible.

4. Stretch arms out wide and yawn. Continue stretching muscles as if warming up to exercise.

5. Slump over at hips, with the top of your head and your arms dangling toward the ground, with your neck relaxed. Bend knees slightly and shake/stretch out any stiff areas.

---

6. Gradually roll spine up, one vertebra at a time, stretching out stiff areas and ensuring relaxation at each level. Shoulders and head should roll up last.

7. Once upright, imagine a string attached at the top of your head, pulling you toward the ceiling. Place your feet shoulder width apart. Align knees, hips, and shoulders comfortably over your feet.

8. Sway gently back and forth to maintain flexibility, keeping the image of a string attached to the top of your head, pulling you upward.

9. Keep the back of your neck lengthened, and prevent your chin from thrusting forward when you speak.

Alignment Exercise—Sitting

1. Sit down toward the edge of a chair, with your knees slightly apart.

2. Roll your head gently from one shoulder to the other and back.

3. While looking at the floor, stretch your arms high into the air, grasping with your fingertips at the highest point.

4. Stretch arms out wide and yawn. Continue stretching muscles as if warming up to exercise.

5. Slump over at hips and dangle the top of your head and your arms toward the ground over your chair, with your neck relaxed.

6. Gradually roll spine up, one vertebra at a time, stretching out stiff areas and ensuring relaxation at each level. Shoulders and head should roll up last. Don't rely on the back of the chair for support.

7. Once upright, imagine a string attached at the top of your head, pulling you toward the ceiling.

8. Keep the back of your neck lengthened, and prevent your chin from thrusting forward when you speak.

Quick Alignment Exercise—Standing

1. Stand up. Imagine a string attached at the top of your head, pulling you toward the ceiling. Place your feet shoulder width apart. Align knees, hips, and shoulders comfortably over your feet.

2. Sway gently back and forth to maintain flexibility, as if you were a tennis player awaiting a serve.

3. Stand upright. Roll shoulders back and down.

Quick Alignment Exercise—Sitting

1. Sit down toward the edge of a chair with your knees slightly apart.

2. Imagine a string attached at the top of your head, pulling you toward the ceiling.

3. Roll shoulders back and down.

4.3.2 Core Strengthening

You need muscular strength to support proper breathing. Strengthening your core also helps you portray confidence and command through an athletic posture. Megan Brown (Doctor of Physical Therapy and Polestar Certified Practitioner of Pilates for Rehabilitation, founder and owner of *Mind the Mat* Pilates studios in Alexandria, Virginia) spends her days strengthening her clients' core. Try her exercises to improve yours.

Wall Slides Exercise

1. Stand against a bare wall, with feet slightly away from wall. Points of contact with the wall should be:

    *   back of head;

    *   upper back between the shoulder blade;

    *   bottom.

2. Raise arms in a "W" position, placing the elbows and the back of the hands against wall (if they don't reach the wall, work toward this goal or *see* "Door Stretch").

3. Slide arms up and down the wall within a small range at first.

Key points for set up:

    *   Stand as tall as you can, reaching the back, top area of your head toward ceiling.

    *   Make sure tops of shoulders are out of the ears—"feel a long space from ear lobes to tops of shoulders." To create resistance,

---

imagine your arms are moving through molasses as you glide them up and down the wall.

- Keep upper chest lifted and collar bones "wide."

- Pull abdominals and front rib cage in.

- Breathe with side and back rib cage (these are the intercostal muscles mentioned earlier).

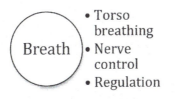

My best voice teachers began each lesson with breathing exercises. Good breathing is essential for a good quality voice. Good breathing also calms nerves. The muscles used to breathe deeply help regulate the flow of air you send to your larynx to control volume and modulate the tone of your voice.

Most attorneys have shallow breathing habits. Switching to deep and wide breathing changes the way they sit, stand, and talk. It also adds an unexpected career bonus—it helps protect and enhance the quality of the voice. We could sing or speak for twenty-four hours a day if we fueled the voice with breath and focused the voice in the facial mask. Breathing is sensing the muscular belt under and around the rib cage. When we expand and contract the torso muscles, air is delivered to the larynx to stabilize the voice. This makes your voice clearer, stronger, and more controlled. These qualities are essential to your success.

When you begin working on your torso breathing, it might feel unnatural until you develop and use muscular control. Once it becomes a habit, managing your breathing is easier and more natural. Torso breathing helps you move the right amount of air steadily through the larynx, and place sound into the facial mask.

This steadiness will ease your nerves and contribute to a better performance. I remember starting my first acting classes in New York lying on the floor of the studio trying to stay calm with breathing exercises. With deeper inhalation, you can slow and lengthen your exhalation. This tells the hypothalamus to release hormones that reduce the production of stress hormones and help relaxation. Thinking also becomes clearer as more oxygen is pumped to your brain.

Voice quality and endurance improve as you harness your breath. The first exercises described below use and strengthen the muscles that control the breath support system for your voice. They also lower anxiety through breath control.

4.3.3 *Torso Breathing*

Find Your Diaphragm Exercise—Standing

1. Stand with vertical alignment.

2. Roll shoulders back and down.

3. Lift rib cage and place one hand under rib cage on your diaphragm area.

4. Blow all air out on a "sh" sound (do not let your rib cage collapse).

5. Without taking a breath, pinch nose and hold breath for five seconds.

6. With chest lifted, inhale through the nose and feel the expansion under in and under the rib cage.

Finding Your Diaphragm Breathing Exercise—Sitting

1. Sit toward the edge of your chair with vertical alignment.

2. Roll shoulders back and down.

3. Lift rib cage and place one hand under rib cage on your diaphragm area.

4. Blow all air out on a "sh" sound (do not let your rib cage collapse).

5. Without taking a breath, pinch nose and hold breath for five seconds.

6. With chest lifted, inhale air through the nose and feel the expansion in and under the rib cage.

Wake Up the Torso—Standing

1. Stand with vertical alignment.

2. Roll shoulders back and down.

3. Lift chest and place hands under rib cage.

4. Exhale on a quick "ha-ha-ha-ha-ha" sound, feeling the diaphragm pulsate. (Feel the muscle area contracting and expanding quickly.)

Wake Up the Torso—Sitting

1. Sit with proper alignment toward the edge of a chair.

2. Roll shoulders back and down.

3. Lift chest and place hands under rib cage.

4. Exhale on a quick "ha-ha-ha-ha-ha" sound, feeling the diaphragm pulsate.

4.3.4 Nerve Control

Audiences sense nerves immediately. Speakers are paralyzed by anxiety. Nerves keep many excellent attorneys away from the lead role on conference calls and in meetings. Learning to reduce, manage, and control nerves is essential. There are many levels of anxiety, so there are many different kinds of exercises to reduce stress and relax. Michelle Blake, a personal trainer, knows how to calm down her busiest clients:

> Exercise in almost any form can act as a stress reliever. Just getting up and moving around is a powerful way to reduce stress. Exercise allows our muscles to move, encourages blood flow, and boosts our feel-good endorphins, which help us cope with daily stressors. Most importantly, exercise gets us breathing deeper, which triggers the body's relaxation response.

> While all forms of exercise from aerobics to yoga can act as a stress reliever, certain yoga poses are excellent at relieving anxiety and triggering the body's natural relaxation response. Yoga is known for its stress relieving properties and the benefits of yoga include decreased tension, increased strength and balance, increased flexibility, lowered blood pressure and reduced cortisol levels. Chair Corpse Pose is a highly effective pose for rapid stress relief and peace of mind.

Chair Corpse Pose

1. Lie on the floor with your back down and your calves resting on a chair seat.

2. Relax your arms by your sides with your palms facing up.

3. Cover your eyes with a small towel or other soft piece of fabric and insert earplugs if you wish.

4. With each inhalation and exhalation, relax a little bit more. Stay in this position as long as you like; you may even fall asleep.

Corpse pose is the perfect way to begin the relaxation process. This pose is done for complete relaxation of the entire body. It quiets your mind and helps relieve stress.

(Michelle Blake, M.S., NASM & ACSM Certified Personal Trainer, Mblake14@hotmail.com, Blake Strength, LLC, Exercise. Eat. Excel, www.BlakeStr3ngth.com)

What if you don't have time to lie down on your office floor? What if you are just standing up to deliver a presentation or speaking up on a phone call, and anxiety attacks? Here are a few tips to compose yourself when the adrenaline wreaks havoc:

1. Practice your opening until you know it cold. Practice the first minute until it pushes past simple memorization and moves into a natural, adaptable delivery. Memorize the opening with specific movements, as described in the next chapter, which will sear the memorized portion in your brain.

2. Stretch and relax the back of your throat. As you get nervous, the voice box rises and your voice tenses. It's OK to pause for a moment and yawn with your mouth closed to release the tension.

3. Lower your pitch for the first few sentences. When you are nervous, your voice tends to shake and expose your nerves with a quivering sound. Lowering the overall pitch of your voice for the first few sentences makes it harder for your voice to shake. Once you feel that rush of adrenaline pass, you can pop back into your normal pitch.

4. Breathe deeply before you speak. If someone is introducing you or you anticipate speaking at a meeting, take deep breaths to calm your nerves while the current speaker finishes a thought.

5. Slow down. Once you start speaking, take more time than you think necessary to deliver the first minute of your opening. When anxiety hits, you will tend to speed up, and you run the risk of losing your audience when your pace is too fast. Slow down and focus on set pauses.

6. Spread out your opening bullet points in front of you. No one will care or notice if you use notes. Some speakers find that nerves are calmed just by knowing the text is near. I recommend having your speaking points in front of you and a longer, organized, detailed version in a folder. If you are asked a question and you need the detailed version, it is there for you.

7. Ask the audience for a moment for you check your notes to make sure you covered all of your points. Taking a few seconds to concentrate on breathing and calm yourself helps center your alignment and clear your head.

4.3.5 Regulation

You begin regulating your voice by learning to deliver continual air flow to the larynx. Doing so allows you to use your voice more effectively. Audiences suffer through speeches, quickly bored because speakers fail to maintain the audience's interest by manipulating the quality of their voice. Building breath capacity helps you control the pitch, range, speed, and comprehension of your speech. The following two breath regulation exercises, provided by Kate Burke, Associate Professor, and voice and speech specialist at the University of Virginia, develop the deep inhalation and extended exhalation that facilitate the effective speaking of any persuasive text.

Locate and Strengthen Core Muscles—Standing

1. Stand with vertical alignment.

2. Roll shoulders back and down.

3. Lift chest.

4. Take a deep breath, and exhale on an "f" sound for ten seconds. Do not let your rib cage collapse.

5. Increase your exhale time to fifteen, twenty, then twenty-five seconds.

6. Try sustaining your vowel sounds in the same fashion ("a, e, i, o, u").

7. Try walking or jogging while doing this exercise, building up your strength by increasing your exhale timess.

(If this exercise is too difficult, stand with your back against a wall and feel the diaphragm and rib muscles expanding and contracting.)

Locate and Strengthen Core Muscles—Sitting

1. Sit with vertical alignment without relying on the back of a chair for support, with knees slightly bent and feet resting on the floor.

2. Roll shoulders back and down.

3. Lift chest.

4. Take a deep breath, and exhale on an "f" sound for ten seconds. Do not let your rib cage collapse.

5. Increase your exhale time to fifteen, twenty, then twenty-five seconds.

6. Sustain the vowel sounds in the same fashion ("a, e, i, o, u").

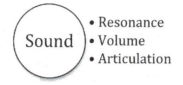

Sound
• Resonance
• Volume
• Articulation

Once you improve your breathing, you should begin to hear changes in the sounds you produce. Your voice can be undermined by many influences—illness, strain, and limited fluid intake. You have control over the overall sound quality, barring these outside influences. When you describe someone as having a richness to their voice, you probably are recognizing good resonance. Resonance is the play of vibrations in and off resonators in the human body. As the sound waves leave your larynx, they vibrate in your resonators—bone, tissue, cartilage.

A good speaker can manipulate resonance by placing the sound in different areas. While you may not easily detect good resonance, you can immediately spot its absence. Some of the vocal problems that arise when the speaker isn't resonating properly include nasal, breathy, brassy, or airy voices. Attorneys should not ignore these problems. Resonance problems are accentuated on phone calls, and most attorneys spend hours taking calls.

The main resonating areas are your head, nasal/sinus cavities, and chest. Most voices can be lumped into one of these categories. By altering the focus of your resonance, you can change the tone of your voice. Ideally, you should resonate from all chambers, placing your voice in them as needed for effect. It is important to figure out if you naturally have a "chest voice" (low, deep resonation), "throat voice" (middle pitched voice), or a "head voice" (thinner, tinny resonation). The best speakers learn to integrate all three.

The resonance exercises aim to identify deeper resonance in your voice, using a perhaps undiscovered natural, built-in speaker system to improve the sound of your voice. In general, I find that volume and articulation problems for attorneys can be solved in the short-term with proper awareness and hard work. It might feel exhausting to project your voice fully enough for the audience to hear you without strain. You might find your lips, teeth, gums, and tongue a bit worn out after using energy to pronounce words with clarity, but a resonant voice energizes rather than fatigues both speaker and audience.

4.3.6 Resonance

Explore Resonance Exercise[1]

1. Hum an "m" sound and feel the vibrating sensation that fills your face and head, especially if your lips are softly touching and you maintain a cushion of space between your upper and lower teeth.

2. Cup your ears and feel a more intense vibration. (This is resonance. You might be surprised by the robust fullness of the sound.)

3. Practice increasing the intensity of this resonance on the "m" sound. Sustain it on different pitches all the way to the end of your breath, siren the pitch up and down, sing the tune of "Row, Row, Row Your Boat" and wake up your lips and mouth. The more "m" sounds you make and the longer they are sustained, the greater the physical feeling and intensity of the vibration.

4. Explore the same way with voiced consonants "n," "v," "z," "ng," "l," "zh," etc. Practice resonating on these consonants while you drive, take a walk, or do the dishes. Short explorations done more often reinforce the sensation of vibration more than long, exhaustive sessions. Make sure your chin is not thrusting forward as you sustain sound; lengthen the back of your neck and allow your chin to drift back and down.

4.3.7 Volume

Resonance means very little if you can't be heard. You must project enough for the audience to hear you clearly. The amount of projection needed changes depending on audience size, format (telephone versus live), and room acoustics. In general, project more than you think necessary. A listener should not strain to hear you. The audience cannot comprehend what it cannot hear.

I divide volume into two categories: projection and focus. You need to project enough voice or sound to create the right decibel level for the situation. The steadier the flow of air from your lungs, the greater the decibels. To be heard, you also need to focus your voice toward the back wall of the space. Often, when you consult notes too much, your volume vacillates because you are failing to maintain a horizontal vocal focus. You look down on the page and speak a line. Look up from the page. Speak a line. The audience hears two different volumes because you are

---

1. Provided by Professor Kate Burke.

delivering the words in two different directions. This often occurs with a lapel microphone. If you turn your head toward the microphone, volume increases. If you look away, the volume decreases.

Volume Exercise

To work on volume, pick a thirty-second text to practice out loud. Print out the text on a single sheet of paper or notecard in large font. This can be your thirty-second introduction of yourself (*see* chapter three), a legal explanation you repeat often, or a favorite excerpt from literature. I have provided a text below.

> Now and then, in this workaday world, things do happen in the delightful storybook fashion, and what a comfort it is. Half an hour after everyone had said they were so happy they could only hold one drop more, the drop came."

Little Women by Louisa May Alcott

Volume Focus Exercise—Standing

1. Stand with your text in hand.

2. While looking down at the page, read the text out loud at a normal speaking volume.

3. Keeping the volume consistent throughout, read the text again while moving your face up and down off the page. You should simulate vacillating volume due to voice placement focus changes only.

4. Read the text again, focusing your voice only at a distinct point on the wall across from you. To achieve this, you must silently read a phrase or sentence, focus on that point, and repeat the phrase or sentence aloud. Continue through the text until it ends.

5. At times in legal practice, you must read text verbatim for the record. Practice this possible on-the-spot read-aloud. Focus on one distinct point across the room.

Volume Focus Exercise—Sitting

1. Sit at a table or desk with your text in hand.

2. While keeping your face looking down at the page, read the text out loud at a normal speaking volume.

---

3. Keep the volume consistent throughout, read the text again while moving your face up and down off the page. Simulate vacillating volume by only changing voice placement focus changes.

4. Read the text again, focusing your voice at a single, distinct point on the wall across from you. To achieve this, silently read a phrase or sentence, pick up your head, focus on that point, and repeat the phrase/sentence aloud. Continue through the text until it ends.

5. At times in legal practice, you must read text verbatim for the record. Practice this possible on-the-spot read-aloud. Focus on one distinct point across the room.

Projection/Resonance Exercise[2]

1. Activate your mouth and lips by practicing this sequence of words: "Woo, Woe, War, Wow." Your lips should softly, but specifically shape the words rather than have your jaw and teeth "chewing" the words. Repeat each word, several times, allowing the vowel sounds to fill the mouth.?

2. Complete a "speaking scale" on an "m" sound. Sustain an "m" on a medium pitch and slide it up a half-tone or a whole tone, holding the sound comfortably to the end of a breath. Breathe and sustain an "m" sound on that same pitch, but then slide up in pitch again. Repeat, and go up as high as is comfortable. And then come back down to as low a pitch as is comfortable. Don't rush! This exercise is relaxing and can take ten minutes or more. You are training your speaking voice the entire time and experiencing the natural interaction of breath and sound.?

3. Hold an "m" sound on a single pitch in a very nasal, annoying, mosquito-like drone. Staying on the same pitch, segue the sound into rich, full, human vocal resonance. Doing so helps eliminate a scratchy, throaty voice.

4. Sustain an "m" sound and place it in each bony areas of your face and head: upper teeth, bone ridge behind your teeth, nose bone, sinus cavities, forehead, top of head, back of head, sides of head, spinal vertebrae, clavicle, shoulders, ribs, pelvis, arm

---

2. Provided by Professor Kate Burke.

> bones, leg bones, feet bones, and finally all over. Your whole body should be tingling and vibrating—which may take some getting used to!
>
> 5. Chant an "m" on a single pitch as a preface to vowel sounds: "mmm-mmm-ay," "mmmmmm-ee," "mmmmmm-eye," "mmmmmm-oh," "mmmmmm-ooh." Proclaim or speak an "m" sound as a preface to speaking vowel sounds: "mmm-ay!" "mmm-ee!" "mmm-eye!" "mmm-oh!" "mmm-oo!" The longer you sustain the vowel sounds, the freer your voice will be.

4.3.8 Articulation

Another barrier to clear comprehension is the lack of articulation. You must pronounce the words. Crisp consonants frame the vowel sounds, making them—and you—more confident and expressive. In contrast, when you mumble, the essential sound elements of the words elide together, and you appear shy, unconfident, and wavering. Enunciate clearly with crisp consonants. Practice tricky words, especially names.

A note about accents: I love accents, unless they impede my ability to understand you. Accents occur with vowel changes. Think of regional American accents. A New Yorker resonates quick, pithy vowels placed in the sinus cavities. A southern accent extends vowel sounds in a relaxed drawl.

If you speak softly (at low volume), mumble, or have your volume or energy at the ends of phrases, your audience will usually not get what you are saying.

Articulation Exercise

To sharpen your articulation, pick a thirty-second text to practice out loud. Print out the text on a single sheet of paper or notecard in large font. This can be your thirty-second introduction of yourself (*see* chapter three, a legal term you repeat often, or a favorite excerpt from literature). I have provided a text below.

> Friends, Romans, countrymen, lend me your ears! I come to bury Caesar, not to praise him. The evil that men do lives after them, the good is oft interred with the bones; So let it be with Caesar. The noble Brutus Hath told you Caesar was ambitious; If it were so, it was a grievous fault, And grievously hath Caesar answered it.
>
> *Julius Caesar* by Shakespeare

Wake Up Exercise

1. Wake up the muscles and tissues in your face and jaw—begin each by stretching and gently rubbing these tense areas.

2. Take your tongue and run it across your gums.

3. Purse your lips, open mouth wide, move lips to one side and then the other.

4. Make exaggerated facial expressions, stretching your face in different ways.

Tongue Twisters

1. Say the tongue twisters listed below clearly and crisply, first at a moderate rate and then speed up.

2. Try this method with legal words and difficult proper names you encounter in your practice.

   • Toy boat, toy boat, toy boat, toy boat . . . .

   • Unique New York, unique New York, unique New York . . . .

   • Peter Piper picked a peck of pickled peppers, if Peter Piper picked a peck of pickled peppers . . . .

   • I saw Susie sitting in a shoe-shine shop, I saw Susie sitting in a shoe-shine shop . . . .

Lazy to Crisp Exercise

1. Read the text aloud, slurring your consonants and mumbling through the entire text.

2. Read the text aloud, over-enunciating your consonants until you sound punchy and staccato.

3. Read your text aloud with a normal dose of articulation.

An audience connects to the quality or tone of the speaker's voice. Your aim should be to display your instrument's best quality by properly using pitch, range, inflection, rate, and pauses. As you start improving your voice, you will know its limitations and can work on techniques to compensate for the limitations. This is important to your professional advancement, and you will achieve results by paying steady attention to each element.

4.3.9 Pitch

As air moves through your larynx, the vocal folds vibrate. The rate or speed of vibration determines the overall pitch of your voice. Singers classify themselves by voice part—soprano, mezzo soprano, alto, mezzo alto, tenor, baritone, and bass. To keep it simple, classify yourself as having a voice this is generally high pitched, medium pitched, or low pitched.

For the most part, audiences dislike high speaking voices, unless that voice is of such excellent quality that they are drawn to listen to it. A high-pitched voice usually sounds whiney, shrieking, piercing, and diminutive. Women often find themselves limited to a high pitch range.

Men often speak in a low-pitched voices, subconsciously forcing themselves into lower voice to sound more masculine and authoritative. The trouble with low-pitched voices are two-fold: they are hard to hear, and they can easily slip into a monotone drone.

Pitch Exercise

To widen your pitch range, pick a thirty-second text to practice out loud. Print out the text on a single sheet of paper or notecard in large font. This can be your thirty-second introduction of yourself (see chapter three), a legal term you repeat often, or a favorite excerpt from literature. I have provided a text below:

> He closed his eyes, fell to mumbling, and presently
> was silent. After a time, he opened his eyes again, and

---

gazed vacantly around until his glance rested upon the kneeling Lord Chancellor. Instantly his face flushed with wrath.

The Prince and the Pauper by Mark Twain

1. Record yourself reading the text in your normal speaking voice.

2. Listen to the recording. Focus on the high or low quality of your voice.

3. Record yourself reading the text in the highest, squeakiest voice possible. Try to jump to the top notes in your register.

4. Listen to the recording. Focus on the high-pitched tones you may not have heard your voice produce before now.

5. Record yourself reading the text in the lowest, deepest part of your voice. Imagine you are speaking in the basement of your voice.

6. Listen to the recording. Focus on the low-pitched tones you may not have heard your voice produce before now.

7. Record yourself reading the text again in your normal register, but this time stretch to include some of the high and low notes you just explored.

4.3.10 Range

Once you know your own habitual range (high or low), begin noticing whether other speakers cover a wide range of pitches in the course of a conversation or monologue. Actors use a wide range of notes—the wider the range, the more expressive a speaker sounds. A robot's "voice" would have a narrow range of notes, leaving it virtually monotone. A pop singer can cover two to three octaves in a song, covering a wide range of pitches. A good oral communicator speaks with a wide range of pitches, accentuating her voice with high and low pitches as the moment demands. If you find yourself bored or tired when listening to someone speak, they are probably displaying a narrow vocal range. This boring mode of speech dampens the audience's attention.

Stretching your vocal range allows you to express emotion when you are making your presentation and thus help keep the listener's interest. You may find that you have a wider vocal range when standing, since most speakers take advantage of better breathing and posture in a standing position—it gives them the ability to reach higher and lower notes in their voice.

Find Your Range Exercise—Standing

1. Prepare an audio-recording device. While standing in good posture, read the following text aloud and record it:

> Endure nothing from anyone except Monsieur the Cardinal and the king. It is by his courage, please observe, by his courage alone, that a gentleman can make his way nowadays. Whoever hesitates for a second perhaps allows the bait to escape during that exact second fortune held out to him. You are young. You ought to be brave for two reasons: the first is that you are a Garcon and the second is that you are my son. Never fear quarrels, but seek adventures. I have taught you how to handle a sword; you have thews of iron, a wrist of steel. Fight on all occasions. Fight the more for duels being forbidden, since consequently there is twice as much courage in fighting. I have nothing to give you, my son, but fifteen crowns, my horse, and the counsels you have just heard."

(*Three Musketeers*, by Alexandre Dumas)

2. Listen to the recording to accustom your ear to the high and low pitches you reach in the reading.

3. Record the text again, this time using a monotone pitch throughout.

4. Record the text again, this time using the widest range you can muster. Try to sound overblown and cartoonish.

5. Listen to both the monotone and the wide-range versions.

6. Record the text a final time, using an expressive, but realistic range of notes.

4.3.11 Inflection

Your voice stretches to different pitches, covering a range of notes. Speakers create patterns of speech depending on when they cause their voices to fall in pitch at the end of clauses, phrases, and sentences. Imagine a "bossy voice," full of deflections in pitch at the end of each phrase. This voice barks a command with every descent in pitch. Now imagine someone who sounds insecure and uncertain about his position, questioning each phrase with an upward turn in pitch. In America, some refer to this repetitive upward inflection as a "Valley girl" voice.

After years of coaching, I continue to find countless attorneys who cannot properly inflect and descend in pitch at the proper time. To do this appropriately, you need to understand the proper use of operative words. Operative words are words stressed or accentuated to convey meaning. When you speak, you "make points" by stressing operative words. Say the following sentence out loud: "The bank will close the deal in October." Your voice determines the operative words in the sentence for the listener. If timing is important, you would stress the word *October.* Say the sentence with that word stressed. If the finality of the deal is important, you could stress *close the deal.* Stressed words become the "operative words" in any sentence. You can accentuate operative words by changing volume, altering pitch, or placing operative words between pauses.

For your voice to inflect expressively, you must inflect it up somewhere in a sentence so your voice can descend at the end of the sentence. To drop the tentative upward inflection pattern, you must train your voice to inflect on operative words within the sentence. This process of breaking an irregular speech pattern takes time and practice. If you notice you have a repetitive, predictable, questioning upward inflection or a repetitive, predictable, condescending deflection, try the following:

1. Sensitize your ear to good structure and proper audible expression by listening to great actors read good literature. Many audio books contain performances by reputable actors who express proper inflection patterns.

2. Over-correct your pattern until you have a balanced approach. For example, if you have misplaced upward inflections, practice speaking with an overabundance of declines in pitch at the ends of phrases.

3. Prepare presentations using the "Operative Words" technique outlined in chapter six.

Upward Inflection Detection

1. While recording yourself with an audio device, introduce yourself, your firm, and speak a few sentences about the type of law you practice.

2. Listen back for the upward ticks in your voice, places where you rise in pitch.

3. Record yourself again, accentuating the end of each phrase with an upward inflection. You should sound like each phrase is a question.

4. Listen to the "upward inflection" recording.

---

5. Record yourself again, accentuating the end of each phrase with a decline in pitch. You should turn each phrase into a strong statement of fact.

6. Listen to the factual statement.

7. Record yourself again, this time trying to deliver a balanced introduction, with proper inflection on stressed words and pitch descent on phrase endings.

8. Listen to the "balanced" recording to check for proper pitch rise and fall.

9. Repeat the same process with the following text (this text demands a commanding voice, dominated by pitch descents):

   > I take no leave of you, Miss Bennet. I send no compliments to your mother. You deserve no such attention. I am most seriously displeased.

   (*Pride and Prejudice*, by Jane Austen)

10. Repeat the same process with the following text (this text demands a questioning tone, dominated by upward inflections):

    > I take no leave of you, Miss Bennet. I send no compliments to your mother. You deserve no such attention. I am most seriously displeased.

    (*Pride and Prejudice*, by Jane Austen)

4.3.12 Speed

Speed is where advanced advocacy takes flight. Crafting the pace of a piece is essential to success, but balancing the fast and slow segments is an art. You can learn how to shape the piece by using speed. There are several guideposts to speed that every attorney should know:

1. Audiences dislike slow speakers. First, the audience gets bored. Second, they feel like the speaker is being condescending when the pace is too slow.

2. Audiences often get lost with fast speakers. If the pace of a speaker is too fast, the audience turns off. The rate of speed must be at a digestible pace for messages to flow into the listener's mind. A fast speaker also runs the risk of sounding over-rehearsed and robotic.

3. Increasing your speed in a list or series makes it sound like you would have more facts to list if time permitted. If you have a chance to list a series of accomplishments or facts in your favor, speeding through them makes the listener think there are endless examples waiting in the wings. Slowly defining things makes them sound singular and finite.

4. In storytelling, talking faster builds momentum. Remember, the audience does not recall every part of a story. You control the audience's memory by paying attention to speed and stylistic techniques. For example, speed through unimportant facts and slow down and insert pauses in portions that you want the audience to remember.

Speed Exercise

1. Read the following text aloud. Record it, then listen back for the overall speed. Keep track of your overall time. This piece should take about forty-five seconds to read properly.

   > But I had not time to be of help. The wrestler dropped at last; and Alan, leaping back to get his distance, ran upon the others like a bull, roaring as he went. They broke before him like water, turning, and running, and falling one against another in their haste. The sword in his hands flashed like quicksilver into the huddle of our fleeing enemies; and at every flash there came the scream of a man hurt. I was still thinking we were lost, when lo! They were all gone, and Alan was driving them along the deck as a sheep-dog chases sheep.

   > *Kidnapped* by Robert Louis Stevenson

2. After mapping out when you want to increase and decrease speed, record yourself reading the text again.

3. Repeat this exercise with your thirty-second introduction.

Group Voice Exercise: Speed and Inflection

Present a thirty- to sixty-second personal description to a small group. Listen for appropriate speed and vocal inflection.

Presenter	Appropriate speed	Appropriate upward and downward vocal inflection	Successes and improvement recommenda-tions

4.3.13 Pauses

Pausing equals power. Imagine being in a boardroom with a CEO. The CEO speaks like a scared rabbit, covering time with needless fillers, "uh," "eh," "ah." Now imagine a different CEO, who projects confidence with silent moments. Pausing makes us wait for the speaker. It allows us to digest the information just given. Pausing also cushions those words the speaker wants remembered. Pausing is essential.

1. Shed the fillers. If you want to persuade and lead, get rid of the annoying fillers that clog the airways. Pausing for a brief time to think projects much more confidence.

2. Use pauses sparingly. Pauses are powerful. Not every moment should be buffered by them. So you must make hard choices and decide which moments deserve attention worthy of a pause.

3. Start reading poetry again. The meter, cadence, and pauses in poetry emit the meaning and emotion in a brief span of time. In *The Gospel in Slow Motion*, Ronald Knox describes the power of poetry:

    > Richard Crashaw, one of the greatest of our English Catholic poets, went in as an undergraduate at Cambridge for a Latin poetry prize; and the subject he was told to write on was the miracle at Cana of Galilee. And at the end of the three hours he showed up with one line, which means, "The shame-faced water saw its Lord, and blushed." He got the prize.

Poetry contains big and small ideas and pictures in few words. Even when the poem is in broken meter, reading poetry teaches how to use a pause to elicit the poet's meaning. Cicero recommended practicing with poetry precisely to learn how to handle meter, time, pacing, and pauses.

Pause Exercise

1. Record yourself reading the following text; keep a steady pace without pausing.

    Shall I compare thee to a summer's day?

    Thou art more lovely and more temperate:

    Rough winds do shake the darling buds of May,

    And summer's lease hath all too short a date:

    Sometime too hot the eye of heaven shines,

    And often is his gold complexion dimmed,

    And every fair from fair sometime declines,

    By chance, or nature's changing course untrimmed:

    But thy eternal summer shall not fade,

    Nor lose possession of that fair thou ow'st,

    Nor shall death brag thou wander'st in his shade,

    When in eternal lines to time thou grow'st,

    So long as men can breathe, or eyes can see,

    So long lives this, and this gives life to thee.

    (Sonnet XVIII, William Shakespeare)

2. Read and record the sonnet again, mapping out ahead of time the moments that demand a pause. Listen for the increased meaning and impact.

3. Read and record your thirty-second introduction from chapter three. Insert pauses at the appropriate times to craft the memory of the audience.

4.4   How to Dive In

As you practice the exercises in this chapter, your vocal strengths and weaknesses will reveal themselves. Pick your weakest element—or seek counsel from a trusted advisor—to begin improving. When I asked Professor Kate Burke from the University of Virginia's Department of Drama what three things she would have an attorney improve to create a confident, persuasive voice, she recommended:

1. I would shift a voice stuck in the throat definitively forward, cultivating focus/placement/resonance in our natural woofers and tweeters: the bony areas of the facial mask. A gravelly voice is the single most pervasive problem I have encountered in [nearly forty] years of voice teaching and coaching.

2. I would re-activate every speaker's lips, relaxing them forward to give subtle shaping and visual impact to consonant sounds and major vowel sounds. Most mouths are stuck in a tense, sideways, pre-smile position that increases nasality. Softly rounded and forward lip shaping makes a voice articulate and expressive and acts as a natural microphone.

3. I would eradicate the pernicious habit of upwardly inflecting the end of definitive statements of fact. This upward slide transforms facts into weak, apologetic questions. Coupled with the fillers "um," "like," and "you know," this Valley-speak inflection masks a speaker's maturity, experience, education, and cognitive complexity. What a loss!

Voice and speech pattern improvements should happen one at a time. You might find that as you improve one area, another reaps the benefits of your hard work. Use the table provided to start your progress. Try focusing on one new goal until you form new habits that change the sound and quality of your voice.

Short-Term Goals	Long-Term Goals
Posture—Alignment	Posture—Core strength
Breath—Nerve Control	Breath—Diaphragm
Sound—Volume	Breath—Regulation
Sound—Articulation	Sound—Resonance
Quality—Range	Quality—Pitch
Quality—Speed	Quality—Inflection
	Quality—Pauses

CHAPTER FIVE

BODY LANGUAGE

"People pay more to be entertained than educated."

—Johnny Carson

Body language, used in concert with your well-crafted message and voice, is a powerful persuasion tool. Nonverbal communication includes your stance or seated posture, poise, eye contact, overall energy, gestures, and facial animation. Body language nonverbally communicates feeling and meaning.

Using this tool is hard for most of us. Sometimes we are not comfortable in our skin. The virtues of humility, self-control, and fortitude must exist to conquer the fear of public speaking . . . plus a bit of grit. The fear of public speaking (glossophobia) is partly a fear of failure. For many, the fear becomes greater as they worry about what to do with their bodies when they are speaking. This chapter focuses on effective body language techniques that will enhance your oral communications. These techniques also help you overcome glossophobia.

First, assess how you currently look and behave. Your video camera or smartphone will be essential. As you read this chapter, make the video recordings I recommend, and flip it to the TV or your tablet where you can review it. At the very least, you will spot glaring body language successes and failures. Ask a friend or colleague to review exercises and give you additional feedback.

As you notice problems and set goals for correction, avoid telling yourself to simply stop the offending behavior. Instead, give yourself something better to do in its place. To improve body language, *replace* ineffective motion, posture, or activity instead of eliminating it. I will share the motions, postures, and activities that are ineffective and those that usually work. For example, if you want to stop randomly pacing back and forth, *replace* the pacing with deliberate movement at key moments in a presentation. If you want to stop an overused repetitive gesture, *replace* the gesture with specifically chosen and timed alternatives. If you want to correct an awkward brooding expression, *replace* it with an appropriate cheerful expression.

We come in all shapes and sizes, with different energy levels and a variety of backgrounds. Because of this diversity, strive to feel natural in a way that is suitable for the space and audience. Think of the space and audience varying the intensity of body language. If you are speaking in a cavernous ballroom, your body language needs to intensify and open up—gestures wider, expressions amplified, posture more energized. Otherwise, you will be lost in the space. If you are sitting across the dinner table from your audience, tone down the intensity of your body language. Huge or constant gestures will distract your dinner guest and the message could be lost. Staying natural in a smaller space means minimizing your body language.

Staying natural varies for each person. Teaching how to become natural as a speaker starts with correcting bad habits. Here are guideposts for improvement.

5.1   Find a Few Comfortable "Home Bases"

"Home base" is a calm posture from which gestures flow, allowing you to show passion, confidence, or other appropriate emotion. Each attorney should have a few "go to" seated postures and standing postures. Start noticing your own home bases when you speak to friends and family. Once you find solid home bases when standing and seated, practice transitioning in and out of each home base, eventually gesturing in and between these positions.

For shorter presentations, you may notice that you only need one home base. If you plan on speaking for an extended time, a few home bases help break up the presentation for the audience and keep your body energized for the duration. Remember that audiences need a change approximately every three minutes. Sometimes a presentation will not have logical three-minute breaks in substance, but you can reset the audience's attention by changing your position or home base. Due to the nature of the topic or presentation, shifting your position may be the only change available.

Moving from base to base also prevents you from looking statuesque. Below are some home bases that you should try while you read this chapter. Put the book down and try them. You may have already incorporated some into your presentation style. Others may feel strange until you try them out. You may find that you already have a better one that suits your personality. If so, use it.

Seated Home Bases	
Sitting on edge of chair, aligned posture and hands at mid-torso on table	Casual or formal, excellent way to start off a presentation in seated position. It exhibits good posture and energy.
Leaning back in chair	Use in a casual setting. It is best suitable for discussion time.
Hand holding prop	Casual or formal, the prop can be a writing utensil or remote clicker/ pointer.
Hands holding notes needed for presentation	Casual or formal. Hold notes low to the table. Don't let the notes dominate this or any home base.
Hands clasped on table	Casual or formal. Have no tension in hands; keep air between the fingers to prevent wringing.
Hands set flat on table	Casual or formal. Make sure hands look relaxed in this position.
Leaning in, arms folded on table	This is a casual pose and is suitable for smaller presentation and group discussions.

Standing Home Bases	
Actor's neutral	Casual or formal. Keep body aligned, arms at side, chest lifted. Excellent way to begin a presentation.
Hand in pocket	Casual or formal. It is generally more useful for men, since women's slacks rarely have pant pockets. This home base can purposely be used to make you more approachable.
Hands clasped at mid-torso	Casual or formal. Rest hands just below rib cage. Do not clasp with tension. Keep arms relaxed.

Hand holding a prop	Casual or formal. The prop can be a writing utensil or remote clicker/pointer.
Hands holding notes needed for the presentation when podium is not available	Casual or formal. This should not dominate this or any home base.
Hands resting on either side of a podium	This is formal. Have no tension in hands. Avoid looking like you are holding on to it for balance.
Standing to the side of a podium or table with one hand resting on it	Casual or formal. This is effective for question and answer section, and/or to break up the monotony of a podium position.

5.2   Present Yourself Well from the Start

Audiences interpret your conscious and unconscious body language messages before you open your mouth. First impressions are often made in those first few moments and are hard to shake. When you walk into a room, your gait, carriage, and posture send a message. When you stand before an audience to speak, you are being asked to take command of the room. For the audience to follow your lead, you need to put them at ease—take care of the troops. The posture-correcting exercises mentioned in chapter three will help you use diaphragm breathing to exert a quiet confidence. You can't force an audience to feel comfortable. But if you are comfortable, they will follow your lead. You need to lead the audience with an air of deference.

First Impressions Exercise

1.   Set up a video-recording device.

2.   Practice walking into a room with a confident gait.

3.   Go from a seated to standing position in the front of the room. Practice this.

4.   When seated, switch from being a listener in a room to the speaker in a room and back.

5.   Review the video and look for awkward transitions and positions. Re-record and practice starting from standing and seated positions until you find both successful.

5.3   Do Not Evoke Sympathy

Audiences don't like to feel sorry for the speaker. The speaker who wears his nerves—fiddles with a prop, trembles, paces, or gasps for breath—makes the audience feel compassion for the speaker's failure or perceived weakness, but detracts their attention from the speaker's message. If you know these tendencies overtake you when you stand to speak, you should force yourself into more and more speaking roles until the nerves stop arresting your progress.

"Get Rid of the Worst" Exercise

1.   Record a thirty-second opening from a seated position.

2.   Record a thirty-second opening from a standing position.

3.   Focus on the following problem areas.

4.   Use the table below to keep track of any problem areas and write ideas for a replacement activity. Take one area at a time, focus only on that distracting tendency, and correct the problem by replacing it with some proactive activity. For example, if your hands shake, try different techniques: hold a prop or keep your hands on the podium (standing) or lying flat on the table (sitting) until the shaking subsides.

	Seated Problem Area	Seated Replacement Activity	Standing Problem Area	Standing Replacement Activity
Distracting hand gestures				
Distracting facial expression				
Trembling or shaking				
Rocking back and forth				
Pacing in room				
Audible gasps for breath				

5.4 Respect the Audience's Personal Space

Most of us have an acquaintance in one of our social circles who can't seem to understand the unspoken rule of respecting personal space. Likewise, the audience in a presentation needs you to respect its personal space. Balance your personal frame and size with the audience and room. If you are a 6'5" male, your frame and size can be intimidating. Orators of that size need to maintain a deeper cushion of space toward the audience. Audiences recoil if challenged too aggressively with intrusions into their space. If you are barely five foot, try to take up more space than you are entitled to have. Sit on the edge of your chair in a meeting. Avoid leaning on the table. Choose big gestures that help widen your frame.

5.5 Rank Sets the Mood

In general, follow the rank in the room to set the tone for formality, erring on the side of a mannered presentation. If the CEO wants board members to casually discuss something, resist the urge to stand and present at a podium or in a formal fashion. If the managing partner of your firm prefers PowerPoint presentations, create and deliver one.

5.6 Find Your Tension

Most people have a place where their tension resides—many contract their jaw muscles or hands, for example. Record yourself giving your thirty-second introduction and try to look for your tension areas. Once you have identified them, work on relaxing those areas when you speak. If you notice that you hold tension in your jaw, massage your jaw joint and facial muscles before presenting. If your hands show nerves, stretch them before and during a communication. Use the video to see if this works. I recommend keeping "air between your fingers" as you gesture, so your hands look relaxed (it will also help prevent you from wringing your hands, if that's your tic). Another trick to release hand tension is to clench them, then release the tension. Doing this "tense and release" technique moments before beginning your presentation can channel adrenaline and release the nerves building in that area. You can also use this tense and release exercise for your jaw and face.

5.7 Connect to Your Message

Your posture, gestures, and facial animation should match the energy level of your message. Your body should appear connected to your words. The audience wants to be entertained, so do not be the speaker that makes them struggle to stay interested. Most of us know an acquaintance who acts so subdued in social situations that you wonder if they need an oxygen injection to show some life. Keeping life injected into a presentation takes hard work and planning. Good communicators work hard to keep audiences interested in their message.

Connection Exercise

1. Set up a video-recording device.

2. Record yourself reading the following passage. Resist making any facial expressions and gestures. You should be still physically, but try to be as vocally expressive as possible. Use high volume and a wide vocal range.

    > As the line halted, Napoleon shouted to the drummer-boy, "Beat a retreat!" The boy stepped forward, grasped his drumsticks and said, "Sire, I do not know how. I have never been taught that. But I can beat a charge. Oh! I can beat a charge that will make the very dead fall into line!"

3. Record yourself reading the same passage matching your expressive voice with expressive gestures and facial expressions.

4. Review both recordings. The text demands a forceful voice and body delivery style.

5. Record yourself reading the following passage. Use huge gestures and exaggerated facial expressions.

    > Once or twice in a lifetime we are permitted to enjoy the charm of noble manners, in the presence of men or women who have no bar in their nature, but whose character emanates freely in their word and gesture. A beautiful form is better than a beautiful face; a beautiful behavior is better than a beautiful form: it gives a higher pleasure than statues or pictures—it is the finest of the fine arts.

6. Record yourself reading the same passage. Use subdued gestures and subtle facial expressions.

7. Review both recordings. The text demands a measured voice and body delivery style.

5.8   Know How to Use a Prop

Audiences want to watch you, not a prop. A prop can be a pen, paper, coffee cup, screen projector remote control, or any object you hold in your hand. If you do hold something in your hand, avoid making it a distraction. Sometimes a prop can ground a speaker and help give the body focus and calm. If your hands shake during a presentation, try holding something to stop the shaking. Starting a presentation with something in your hands can calm nerves. You can eventually discard the prop once the initial adrenaline rush has subsided. Use the video to see how a presentation looks with and without a prop.

5.9   Make Genuine Eye Contact

Eye contact is powerful and sensitive. The audience senses when you actually look into the eyes of a listener and when you cheat, looking near or above their eyes. Eye contact means you lock eyes. A large audience can detect whether you make direct eye contact with other audience members. They sense a real connection. In any size audience, eye contact has the added benefit of keeping the attention of all the listeners. Done properly, the entire audience should expect that "I could be next" to be seen and connect with the speaker.

Keep eye contact with someone until you complete a phrase or point or section. Think about eye contact as a way to ensure you have explained yourself, that the audience understands you. Glean information about your own messaging by the way the audience listens—with the following caveat: younger generations are not as talented with good listening skills. A younger audience might completely understand you, but look distracted; they might even be rude enough to check their smartphone during your presentation.[1]

During a one-on-one presentation, you need to handle eye contact sensitively. If you stare too long at someone, you run the risk of crossing into the uncomfortable zone. Instead, allow one another to look away, think, take notes. In a small conference room (eight chairs or fewer), choose a seat that respects rank (do not sit at the head of the table if you are not the highest ranking person at the meeting) and affords you the best vantage point to make eye contact with as many audience members as possible. In that small meeting, make eye contact with everyone in the room, but direct the bulk of your message and eye contact at the appropriate audience members. For example, if you and a team of colleagues deliver a pitch to a team of three in-house counsel, focus your eye contact on the prospective clients, not your colleagues. In a large conference room or auditorium, you may not be able to make eye contact with everyone, so make an effort to connect (eye to eye) with someone in different sections of the room. This makes each audience member feel attended to.

Listen, watch, and learn from the audience. You will never learn how to perceptively read their body language if you don't look them in the eye.

---

1. When I taught law school classes, I required all electronics be turned off in my class to keep students' attention and teach them better listening skills.

Audience Connection Group Exercise

Present a thirty- to sixty-second personal description in conversational style to a small group of colleagues. During each presenter's delivery, others in the group interrupt and ask questions. The goals of this exercise are to 1) actively listen to questions asked, 2) maintain appropriate eye contact with audience members, and 3) answer the questions asked. Use the table below to take notes, discuss successes, and brainstorm ideas for improvement.

Presenter	Listening skills and eye contact	Answers the questions asked	Successes and improvement recommendations

5.10 Use Gestures that Are Natural and Suitable for the Audience and Space

Your gestures should be fluid. They should match your message and intensity. They should, above all, match your personality. Gestures are a powerful tool, allowing you to bring the audience's attention to key points, move the plot forward, and leave the audience with a memorable impression. Gestures also help actors memorize text. To memorize long presentations, add gestures and blocking (directions for the speaker where to move and stand) to help sear the performance in your mind.

Gestures should be connected to the words. Imagine a bad actor trying to perform Shakespeare, throwing out random gestures half a second behind the lines to be illustrated. This disconnected style is uncomfortable to watch and signals that the speaker is fearful or inexperienced.

What gestures should you use? Those that are productive and varied. I disagree with coaches who teach canned, predictable gestures. I generally teach the opposite technique. Vary your gestures so they stay fresh and move the plot forward. If an audience remembers a repeated gesture (karate chopping the podium, wagging a pointed finger), you need to vary those movements. If the audience sees movements that help describe the text, they will understand better and remember more. Once you write a simple text with a chosen format (general to particular, particular to general, enumerative, sensory, chronological, compare/contrast), gestures round out the way you describe your message to the audience.

Actors choose gestures that relate to the set, plot, or the other characters in a scene. Explore different gestures that you organically discover by focusing—one at a time—on the following elements: space (set), text (plot), and audience.

Divide the Space Exercise

1. Record and review yourself reading aloud the following text. Sit at a table or stand at a podium where you can have the text close by. Your hands should be free to move when you feel inspired to do so. Pretend there is one person sitting opposite you.

Choices and Change

Mrs. George Bush

Former First Lady of the United States

June 1, 1990—Severance Green, Wellesley College, Wellesley, Massachusetts

At the end of your life, you will never regret not having passed one more test, not winning one more verdict or not closing one more deal. You will regret time not spent with a husband, a friend, a child or a parent.

We are all in a transitional period right now . . . fascinating and exhilarating times . . . learning to adjust to the changes and the choices we . . . men and women . . . are facing. I remember what a friend said, on hearing her husband lament to his buddies that he had to babysit. Quickly setting him straight my friend told her husband that when it's your own kids it's not called babysitting!

Maybe we should adjust faster, maybe slower, but whatever the era . . . whatever the times, one thing will never change: fathers and mothers, if you have children they must come first. Your success as a family . . . our success as a society depends not on what happens at the White House, but on what happens inside your house.

2. Record yourself delivering the text again in the same posture (seated or standing). This time, divide the physical space in front

---

of you. Deliver the speech using gestures in different areas of the space in front of you. Try picking three sharp areas—left, right, center—and complete your movements within each area.

Divide the Text Exercise

1. Record and review yourself reading aloud the following text. Sit at a table or stand at a podium where you can have the text close by, but your hands should be free to move when you feel inspired to do so.

Duty, Honor, Country

General Douglas MacArthur

May 12, 1962; West Point, New York

You are the leaven which binds together the entire fabric of our national system of defense. From your ranks come the great captains who hold the nation's destiny in their hands the moment the war tocsin sounds. The Long Gray Line has never failed us. Were you to do so, a million ghosts in olive drab, in brown khaki, in blue and gray, would rise from their white crosses thundering those magic words: *Duty, Honor, Country*.

This does not mean that you are war mongers. On the contrary, the soldier, above all other people, prays for peace, for he must suffer and bear the deepest wounds and scars of war. But always in our ears ring the ominous words of Plato, that wisest of all philosophers: "Only the dead have seen the end of war."

The shadows are lengthening for me. The twilight is here. My days of old have vanished, tone and tint. They have gone glimmering through the dreams of things that were. Their memory is one of wondrous beauty, watered by tears, and coaxed and caressed by the smiles of yesterday. I listen vainly, but with thirsty ears, for the witching melody of faint bugles blowing reveille, of far drums beating the long roll. In my dreams I hear again the crash of guns, the rattle of musketry, the strange, mournful mutter of the battlefield.

> But in the evening of my memory, always I come back
> to West Point. Always there echoes and re-echoes: *Duty,*
> *Honor, Country*.

2. Record yourself delivering the text again in the same posture (seated or standing). Use the meaning in the text to generate gestures. An easy way to do this is to think about the format of the piece (general to particular, particular to general, enumerative, sensory, chronological, or compare and contrast). The format suggests constructive gestures for you to use to keep moving the plot forward. For example, if you have a chronological format, you can use gestures in front to form a timeline. Try moving your hands at torso level, horizontally from right to left (displaying the timeline for the perspective of the audience) to indicate time progression or facts set in time. In "Duty, Honor, Country," there is a clear compare and contrast for you to try.

Divide the Audience Exercise

1. Record and review yourself reading aloud the following text. Sit at a table or stand at a podium where you can have the text close by, but your hands should be free to move when you feel inspired to do so.

Martin Luther King

Indira Gandhi, Prime Minister of India

Speech at the Presentation of the Jawaharlal Nehru Award for International Understanding to Coretta Scott King, New Delhi, India, January 24, 1969

While there is bondage anywhere, we ourselves cannot be fully free. While there is oppression anywhere, we ourselves cannot soar high. Martin Luther King was convinced that one day the misguided people who believed in racial superiority would realize the error of their ways. His dream was that white and black, brown and yellow would live and grow together as flowers in a garden with their faces turned towards the sun. As you yourself said, "All of us who believe in what Martin Luther King stood for, must see to it that his spirit never dies". That spirit can never die. There may be setbacks in our fight for the equality of all men. There may be moments of gloom.

> But victory must and will be ours. Let us not rest until the equality of all races and religions becomes a living fact. That is the most effective and lasting tribute that we can pay to Dr. King.
>
> 2. Record yourself delivering the text again in the same posture (seated or standing). This time, divide the speech into four sections (at logical breaks) and the audience into three sections (A, B, and C). Deliver the first quarter of the speech to the center section (B). Deliver the second quarter of the speech to the stage left section (A). Deliver the third quarter of the speech to the stage right section (C). Deliver the final quarter to the center section (B). Use your hands to relate with the imaginary audience. Review the video and notice how you moved to relate with the audience. At the very least, you should shift your body and gesture to each section of the audience.

One way to gesture more naturally in a presentation is to study your own physical behavior when you are not in the spotlight. Most of the time, you will be natural and suitable if you act as you would around your friends or family. Attorneys suffer from "performance split personality"—they are sure of themselves and behave comfortably in a casual situation, but when the spotlight is on, they become something different and thus awkward. Pay attention to your gesture patterns and choices when you talk on the phone or have dinner at home. Ask a friend or family member to comment on these patterns and choices. When you practice using video and present something in a professional setting, try to mimic your casual self.

5.11 Use Movement Purposefully

Move with purpose in the space given. Audiences enjoy movement, but aimless motion is distracting. If you feel the instinct or the urge to move, do so for a given reason: move to address a different part of the audience, move to interact with a graphic, move towards your notes. A director tells an actor where to start and when to move. These instructions are called blocking—blocking out a scene gives the actor direction on the stage. Similarly, block out your own presentation. If you are sitting, you can block out when to pass out your handout, when to address different sides of the board room, and when to connect with key decision-makers in the room. If you are standing, you can block when you cross from one side of the room to another, when you approach the screen behind you, and when you move away from the podium. Planned blocking helps your presentation have structure and increases how much text you can memorize. Blocking, by moving you with purpose, also stops your rocking and pacing from distracting the audience.

5.12 Interact with Visual Aids Properly

The audience is there to see and hear you. Keep the audience focused on you, and let the graphics be the backdrop.

- Don't let your visual aids overshadow you. Choose visual aids that have few words and allow you to maintain top billing.

- As a general rule, keep your torso facing the audience. If you need to add something to a flip chart or write something on a blackboard, pause to write while your back is turned.

- Plan your visual aids to help you block the presentation. A visual aid allows you to move across a wider area of the table in front of you or the walking space in a room. Plan to move towards the visual aid, interact with it, then plan to move back towards the audience.

- Use a visual aid if gestures are not your forte. Using a visual aid forces your body to do something. Turn the paper of a flip chart. Pass out handouts at a meeting that the audience can follow. Approach a PowerPoint and gesture towards important phrases.

CHAPTER SIX

ACTING FOR ATTORNEYS

*"The actor has to develop his body. The actor has to work on his voice.
But the most important thing the actor has to work on is his mind."*

— *Stella Adler*

6.1 The Likability Factor

The smartest attorney is not always the best attorney, having brains does not mean you are a good communicator, and being brilliant does not guarantee success. To be successful, attorneys need to communicate with power, confidence, and feeling. Emotions and attorneys are not always the best of friends—finding the right pathos is an afterthought for some attorneys. In the appropriate situation, however, the right dose of emotion can often win the day over a well-reasoned stiffly presented argument. Learning to act expands your ability to express the right emotion. Where appropriate, your smart choice could be an appeal to humanity, a gesture of friendship, an empathetic tone, a frustrated expression, or a brusque challenge.

Still, some attorneys are proudly offended at the idea of an attorney acting. In reality, however, we all act. In most day-to-day activities, we pretend when we behave a certain way or hide our true emotion. When a senior partner or client required or "asked" you to attend a function at 6:00 a.m., you pretended you did not mind and you smiled at the function. You were acting. When the judge berated you in a packed court room for interrupting a witness, you took a deep breath and responded civilly. You were acting. When the client decided to take her business in a different direction that materially changed the agreements you had worked on for months, you pretended to not mind. You were acting. The fact is that attorneys who have a reputation for being "hard to work with" often lack the desire or skills needed to act. They don't play nice. They force their instinctive emotion on the rest of their team instead of responding with reserved emotion or civility. You already act, so let's talk about enhancing your techniques so you can be more persuasive when doing so.

To deliver the right emotion, you must be perceptive enough to sense the emotional needs of the audience. Aristotle knew this and called it pathos. Some say you know the moment is right in your gut. Acting trains you to display that emotion—through the words you write for your presentation, your voice, your body language, or your posture. Now we begin putting things together.

Before you weave the right emotions into a presentation, you need a firm foundation to support your credibility. For an attorney, this foundation is likability. Any emotion you portray is built on likability. If you fail to establish a certain rapport with the audience, you run the risk of being seen as a fake, a charlatan.

One tool psychologists use to measure likability is the concept of "Emotional Quotient" or EQ:

emotional intelligence (*n*).

Intelligence regarding the emotions, especially in the ability to monitor one's own or others' emotions.[1]

How's your EQ? Pathos includes the ever-important EQ or "likability" factor. In the competitive legal arena, most attorneys have the legal acumen and proper level of experience to adequately (and perhaps superlatively) provide legal services. Yet clients gravitate to the attorney she likes to work with—those with a good deskside manner. The likability factor is critical for success in any profession. The self-assessment from chapter two should help you discover your likability factor.[2] Here are some additional questions to consider:

1. Can you control your emotions?

2. Can you easily read the emotions of others?

3. Do your colleagues find you easy to work with?

4. Do you cultivate friendships at work?

If you know that your EQ is low, it's never too late to pump up that score. Even if you find it difficult to pump it up in everyday life, you can at least pump it up temporarily for a meeting, phone call, or presentation. Remember, in every presentation, you must force yourself to connect. Sometimes you need only be warm and engaging. Here are some suggestions to help you reach that goal.

---

1. Thefreedictionary.com.

2. You will notice in this and subsequent chapters call back to a technique or principle covered earlier as you piece together a presentation.

Increase Your Likability	
Connect	1. Research your audience before you arrive or make the call. A quick read of someone's bio or a look at his or her picture on line can help you make a connection. Same school? Same home state? Knowing the audience also helps you anticipate what themes will connect to achieve the super-objective of the presentation. The Internet is an effective tool for this purpose.
	2. Surprise someone with the compliment or introduce yourself by recognizing the person without him or her saying his or her name. This is a great compliment and wins big points. You can do this with a person or a small group, and a little research on the audience that lets you make a few personal comments has the same effect. Good performers research the city in which they perform and use it at the beginning of the concert to connect.
	3. If you are face-to-face with the audience (versus a call), look everyone in the eye and greet them with culturally acceptable friendliness.
	4. Begin with small talk. Before the presentation begins, spend a few moments getting to know the audience. Knowing something about the audience opens up conversation.
	5. Read about current events. To connect with another person, you need to find common ground. If there is nothing in common between the two of you, you can both discuss the latest news. However, don't take positions on the divisive issue (even though you may show empathy or understanding to the audience you represent).
	6. Develop hobbies you can talk about with others. We gravitate towards interesting and talented people. Talk about yourself and your interests in a humble manner,
	7. Ask your audience about their interests and then listen. Use your research comment on something relevant to them. People enjoy talking about themselves. They like to be known. Be friendly and ask about their hobbies and professional life.
	8. Remember things about your clients, coworkers, and colleagues. If your boss at the Department of Justice tells you he started sailing, remember it. Ask about it the next time you see him.

Increase Your Likability	
Warm and Engaging	1. Keep eye contact throughout the presentation. Don't pause to read your notes, especially don't be distracting in the opening (e.g., putting on reading glasses to read notes). Good posture in the standing or sitting position, including home-base positions, means head held high with eye contact.
	2. Be attentive; look for signals. If an audience member looks confused about your message, he or she may not be the only one. Address it, if the audience size and form of the presentation allows. If a message isn't connecting, be flexible and shift to another theme; if the audience is nodding agreement, keep pushing the message and wrap it up.
	3. Smile. Yes, even in a serious presentation, there are appropriate moments to be pleasant and smile.
	4. If appropriate, end the presentation with a cheerful or hopeful tone. At the very least, wish the audience well in their future endeavors or a safe trip home.
	5. Follow up important presentations with a handwritten note. Handwritten notes are so rare, recipients are touched that someone took the time to turn off their smartphone and send a note. Mail it! I recommend every professional have personal stationery—keep it simple.
	6. Be polite and respectful to everyone. This builds your ethos or credibility. If you are rude or disrespectful to restaurant servers or assistants or drivers, you will have a hard time convincing your audience that you are a pleasant individual. Being firm or aggressive is completely appropriate, as long as you attack the matter, not the person. Be respectful and polite.

6.2   Guideposts for Emotion

In any oral communication, your job as an attorney is to make your position desirable. This can be tough with a blatantly unfair position in a negotiation or a particularly cantankerous client. If you face bad odds, the emotional tone of your presentation can lead the audience to believe in you, even if they disagree with your position. The first step is to know the super-objective and then to appreciate the audience. With this, you'll have the platform to design the right pathos to use or adjust the themes you have chosen to sell the super-objective. I have seen many effective ways to sway an audience:

6.2.1 Develop a Stage Presence

Some people have the charisma that pulls all eyes to them. What makes certain people stand out in a crowd and be remembered? I have been asked this question repeatedly. I see certain common threads in presenters who naturally possess stage presence. Most of these threads can be woven into your style.

- Presenters with excellent posture and energy command the room. The exercises listed in the previous chapters will help you increase your core strength, correct alignment, and help breath support. They will also make you appear strong and energetic.

- Audiences watch presenters with fluid, natural gestures and who act smooth in front of a crowd. When your gestures are choppy and your nerves overcome your poise, audiences will abandon you to your private spiral downhill.

- Charismatic speakers dress for the part. Just as actors have costumes, your attire is a tool to use. Do you feel a little uncomfortable when the technician taking your blood is wearing worn, frayed jeans and a wrinkled shirt rather than a clean medical jacket or even scrubs? If you wear flashy or immodest clothing, the audience pays attention wto your attire instead of you. If you dress slovenly or disheveled, audiences don't take you seriously. If you your dress is professional, attractive, and tailored, you look the part of a successful attorney. "Dress for the part" also includes considering the location. If the presentation is at a beach resort, don't present in a bathing suit or a three-piece suit. Do some preparation and check with the event coordinator. Some attorneys may remember a photo of Richard Nixon, who is remembered as stiff and stuffy, taking a relaxing walk on Key Biscayne Beach in a three-piece suit and wing tips! Like it or not, your dress and makeup matter.

- People with stage presence are adaptable and quick on their feet. When something goes wrong in a presentation—have I mentioned that something always goes wrong?—folks with charisma bounce back, cover, recover, and move on. When a charismatic performer blunders a word, he quickly corrects it without embarrassment or laughs at himself.

- Speakers with magnetism control their nerves. Somehow, charming people have a handle on the anxiety that cripples others. Audiences follow those who enter a room with calm confidence.

- Effective speakers seem to connect and care about their audience. A charismatic speaker doesn't simply present a good speech, she communicates an idea by living through an action. She doesn't necessarily feel the emotion she describes, but she is able to help the audience feel that emotion. These speakers build a relationship with the audience with pathos. The great speakers stay present in the moment and truly communicate.

6.2.2 Keep It Small

When actors perform on stage, they transmit emotions across a wide space in an auditorium to the audience. When an actor acts in a movie, the emotional changes are more subtle and understated because the camera is often at close range. You should be like a film actor, showing emotional subtleties, not exaggerated emotional displays intended to reach the folks in the third balcony. Attorneys are hired to think reasonably. Emotions must be reasonably displayed. Avoid the extremes—weakness, bossiness, abrasiveness, and hysterics.

6.2.3 Concentrate on Transitions

When you try new emotions and inject acting techniques into presentations, focus on the transitions from one emotion to another. Reaching back to chapter three, sometimes an emotional transition ends and begins another three-minute segment of attention for the audience. When you settle into an emotion—warm and engaging in an opening, for example—your personality and message will show well. Most attorneys fail to make smooth transitions to the next emotion (e.g. moving from the friendly opening to the serious tone needed to deliver the advice in the next section). When you rehearse before a call, meeting, or formal event, practice the transitions. If you can smooth these out, the presentation will flow with proper pathos.

6.2.4 Enjoy Your Work

One of the most common problems I see is boredom and overall discontent from attorneys when they speak. Make the audience believe the message is important and you want to be there. Give your audience a pleasant experience. No one wants to watch a miserable speaker. Greet your audience with a warm expression and keep the energy level high for their benefit.

Emotion, Body Language, and Facial Animation Group Exercise

Meet with a few colleagues or friends. In the small group, each attorney presents a thirty- to sixty-second personal description. The group identifies moments that are emotional successes as well as areas that need improvement. The achievements each presenter will want to show during their personal description should include 1) good first impression (groomed, professional, confident), 2) energy and enthusiasm, and 3) warm and varied facial expressions. Using the table provided below, decide if each presenter achieved the three goals. Rate each category on a scale of 1 to 5, 5 being the most successful. After each performance, discuss positive ways to improve both areas.

Presenter	First impression, before speaking (1–5)	Overall energy, enthusiasm (1–5)	Warm facial expression, varied appropriately (1–5)	Successes and improvement recommendations

6.3   Learn to Act

Most large cities have excellent acting classes for professionals or beginning actors. If you find your EQ to be low or don't do well on the exercise below, I recommend a beginning acting class or improv class.[3] Attending a once-a-week class for a couple months will be worth the time invested.

Learning how to map the right emotions is key to connecting and then communicating well with your audience. There are many gurus of acting—teachers through time that differed about how to properly portray a role. Followers of these gurus adopt the lessons and continually improve their craft. Achieving an honest, realistic portrayal of emotion becomes a lifelong goal for many actors.

6.3.1   Outside In

Some actors arrive at the right emotion or tone by working from the outside in—these actors take external movements, cues, postures, and expressions, and expect that the physical will instruct the internal to follow suit—e.g., the actor stomps around the room, grimaces his face, shouts his lines, and eventually he actually feels mad. This example is exaggerated, but the process of using the physical to inspire the right interior emotion is incredibly effective. Richard Warner, Professor and Head of Acting at the University of Virginia Department of Drama, offers the following excellent exercise to help experience this "outside-in" approach.

---

3. Amy Johnson Conner, "Improve Training Can Improve Your Trial Skills," *Lawyers Weekly USA* (October 2002).

The Gesture Game

This game works best when a text is fully memorized, but it can also be effective when practicing a unit of a speech after the actor/lawyer has scored the piece.[4]

Object of the Game

To organically invent natural, unpremeditated gestures that will enhance a presentation. This game will provide a player with a deep cache of specific, unique physical ideas to select from as a presentation is being developed.

Process

Speak the words of a memorized text aloud in an easy, conversational tone. Simultaneously keep both of your arms and hands moving *all the time*. The challenge is to illustrate *everything* you say as if you were playing charades or telling a small child a story. Be big and bold. Take, for example, the following sentence:

> There was one time way back when I was a kid when I was always picking on someone.

Your simultaneous gestures might look something like this:

> There was one time [*index finger in the air indicating "one"*] way back [*both hands waving behind you*] when I was a kid [*both hands palms down at your belt to indicate how tall you were*] when I was always picking on someone [*both hands demonstrating picking in the air*].

Practice the passage a number of times in this manner. On each journey through the text, spontaneously begin to select certain gestures that best enhance a particular moment. You may discover that you only need four out of fifty gestures and, most of the time, the gestures will maintain their natural and fresh quality.

6.3.2 Inside Out

On the other side of the debate are actors who work from the inside out—these actors remember a moment in their life that triggers emotional memory, and they expect the physical to follow suit (e.g., the actor remembers when his parent died,

---

4. *See* "Scoring a Text" exercises *infra*.

making him remember the sadness, and the body takes on the external signs of sadness). Professor Warner suggests attorneys explore the "outside-in" method using the following game, with the help of a trusted friend or colleague.

The Inner Film Game

An actor's imagination needs to be exercised every day like a muscle. Actors strengthen and deepen their imagination by first remembering that every bit of information that we process arrives to brain through the senses. Actors who exercise their seeing, listening, tasting, touching, and smelling skills in disciplined, inventive ways invariably have more active imaginations.

Object of the Game

To create a sensory-loaded, imaginative inner film of a speech to help an actor-lawyer connect emotionally with the super-objective.

Process

Begin this game by describing aloud everything you have done that day so far, starting with getting out of bed.

1.   As you begin to describe the details of getting dressed, eating breakfast, etc., invariably your observer can invariably see when your eyes focus on one particular area in space. When you look into an area in space to remember, your observer should point this out to you. Usually this happens when you picture all the details you were describing. That "picturing" is called the inner film.

2.   Now apply this simple day-dreaming process to selected phrases in a text or speech. Begin by picturing an animated image of the speech's first phrase. In the "The Gesture Game," it would be: "There was a time way back when I was a kid . . . ." Create this image with specific, sensory detail. What did this kid look like? Are there any sounds, aromas, colors, even tastes that are conjured? (For example, the sound of a seven-year-old voice or the smell of bubble gum or the bright red of a favorite shirt.)

3.   When your inner film is rich with sensory detail, say the words of the speech phrase aloud. Not every phrase offers an actor the opportunity to create sensory connections. Continue the speech until the next opportunity arises, then stop speaking and create the inner film. When the image is rich with sensory detail, then speak the words aloud that the image describes.

6.3.3 *Personal Preference*

Both methods ("outside-in" and "inside-out") work well—it's personal preference. Try both methods to find a way to communicate emotion effectively. I include additional exercises to help you strengthen your ability to act with appropriate emotions.

"Outside-In" Exercise

1. Read the "Eloquence of Daniel O'Connell," which was a classic elocution speech that at one time every orator used. When you insert emotion this passage, your speaking time will be approximately three minutes. This passage is filled with emotional changes and demands. After reading it, set a super-objective.

Eloquence of Daniel O'Connell

The following extract from Wendell Phillips's lecture on Daniel O'Connell was a great favorite in declamation contests in the early 1900s. Daniel O'Connell, known as "the Liberator," was born in 1775 in Ireland. He studied law and was admitted to the bar in Dublin in 1798. He built up a highly successful practice as a lawyer and dealt with many cases of Irish tenants against English landlords. During the next two decades, he was active in the movement to repeal British laws that penalized Roman Catholics because of their religion. Catholics were barred from Parliament, but O'Connell became the leader of the battle to win political rights for Irish Roman Catholics.

I do not think I exaggerate when I say that never since God made Demosthenes has he made a man better fitted for a great work than Daniel O'Connell. You may say that I am partial to my hero; but John Randolph of Roanoke, who hated an Irishman almost as much as he did a Yankee, when he got to London and heard O'Connell, the old slaveholder threw up his hands and exclaimed: "this is the man, those are the lips, the most eloquent that speak English in my day." And I think he was right.

Emerson says, "There is no true eloquence, unless there is a man behind the speech." Daniel O'Connell was listened to because all England and Ireland knew that there was a man behind the speech—one who could be neither bought, bullied, nor cheated.

And then, besides his irreproachable character, O'Connell had what is half the power of the popular orator; he had a majestic presence . . . . There was something majestic in his presence before he spoke, and he added to it the magnetism and grace that melts a million souls into his. When I saw him he was sixty-five—lithe as a boy, his every attitude a picture, his every gesture grace—he was still all nature; nothing but nature seemed to be speaking all over him. It would have been delicious to have watched him if he had not spoken a word, and all you thought of was a greyhound.

Then he had a voice that covered the gamut. I heard him once in Exeter Hall say, "I send my voice across the Atlantic, careering like a thunderstorm against the breeze, to tell the slave-holder of the Carolinas that God's thunderbolts are hot, and to remind the bondman that the dawn of his redemption is already breaking." You seemed to hear his voice reverberating and re-echoing back to London from the Rocky Mountains. And then, with the slightest possible Irish brogue, he would tell a story that would make all Exeter Hall laugh, and the next moment tears in his voice, like an old song, and five thousand men wept. And all the while no effort—he seemed only breathing.

2. Use your body language to inspire emotions. Try finding emotions from the outside in. Physically inspire yourself to choose three separate emotions. I include the text again, with three choices I made, based on the body language that I used during the delivery.

    I do not think I exaggerate when I say that never since God made Demosthenes has he made a man better fitted for a great work than Daniel O'Connell. You may say that I am partial to my hero; but John Randolph of Roanoke, who hated an Irishman almost as much as he did a Yankee, when he got to London and heard O'Connell, the old slaveholder threw up his hands [BOISTEROUS—*inspired by the gestures with my hands*] and exclaimed: "this is the man, those are the lips, the most eloquent that speak English in my day." And I think he was right.

Emerson says, "There is no true eloquence, unless there is a man behind the speech." Daniel O'Connell was listened to because all England and Ireland knew that there was a man behind the speech—one who could be neither bought, bullied, nor cheated.

And then, besides his irreproachable character, O'Connell had what is half the power of the popular orator; he had a majestic presence . . . . [*PRIDE—inspired by the upright posture when the word "majestic" appeared*] There was something majestic in his presence before he spoke, and he added to it the magnetism and grace that melts a million souls into his. When I saw him he was sixty-five—lithe as a boy, his every attitude a picture, his every gesture grace—he was still all nature; nothing but nature seemed to be speaking all over him. It would have been delicious to have watched him if he had not spoken a word, and all you thought of was a greyhound.

Then he had a voice that covered the gamut. I heard him once in Exeter Hall say, "I send my voice across the Atlantic, careering like a thunderstorm against the breeze, to tell the slave-holder of the Carolinas that God's thunderbolts are hot, and to remind the bond-man that the dawn of his redemption is already breaking." You seemed to hear his voice reverberating and re-echoing back to London from the Rocky Mountains. And then, with the slightest possible Irish brogue, he would tell a story that would make all Exeter Hall laugh [*JOYFUL—inspired by the act of laughing*], and the next moment tears in his voice, like an old song, and five thousand men wept. And all the while no effort—he seemed only breathing.

3. Record yourself performing this speech. Use exaggerated body language, seeing which emotions are inspired. Shoot for three clear emotions. Review your recording and look for sharp emotional changes.

"Inside-Out" Exercise

1. Read "Strike Against War" by Helen Keller. This speech has sharp emotional changes. After reading the passage, set a super-objective.

Strike Against War

Helen Keller

Speech at Carnegie Hall, New York City, January 5, 1916, under the auspices of the Women's Peace Party and the Labor Forum

To begin with, I have a word to say to my good friends, the editors, and others who are moved to pity me. Some people are grieved because they imagine I am in the hands of unscrupulous persons who lead me astray and persuade me to espouse unpopular causes and make me the mouthpiece of their propaganda. Now, let it be understood once and for all that I do not want their pity; I would not change places with one of them. I know what I am talking about. My sources of information are as good and reliable as anybody else's. I have papers and magazines from England, France, Germany and Austria that I can read myself. Not all the editors I have met can do that. Quite a number of them have to take their French and German second hand. No, I will not disparage the editors. They are an overworked, misunderstood class. Let them remember, though, that if I cannot see the fire at the end of their cigarettes, neither can they thread a needle in the dark. All I ask, gentlemen, is a fair field and no favor. I have entered the fight against preparedness and against the economic system under which we live. It is to be a fight to the finish, and I ask no quarter.

2. Use personal memories to conjure emotion relevant to the piece. Try finding emotions from the outside-in, letting the emotions dictate your body language and voice work. Physically inspire yourself to choose three separate emotions. I include the text again, with three choices I made, based on the body language that I used during the delivery.

    [*PITY—recall a time when you felt pitied*] To begin with, I have a word to say to my good friends, the editors, and others who are moved to pity me. Some people are grieved because they imagine I am in the hands of unscrupulous persons who lead me astray and persuade me to espouse unpopular causes and make me the mouthpiece of their propaganda. [*INDIGNANT—recall a time when you felt proud and indignant*] Now, let it be understood once and for all that I do not want their pity; I would not change places with one of them. I know what I am talking about. My sources of information are as good and reliable as anybody else's. I have papers and magazines from England, France, Germany and Austria that I can read myself. Not all the editors I have met can do that. Quite a number of them have to take their French and German second hand. No, I will not disparage the editors. [*SARCASTIC—recall a time when you felt sarcastic*] They are an overworked, misunderstood class. Let them remember, though, that if I cannot see the fire at the end of their cigarettes, neither can they thread a needle in the dark. All I ask, gentlemen, is a fair field and no favor. I have entered the fight against preparedness and against the economic system under which we live. It is to be a fight to the finish, and I ask no quarter.

3. Record yourself performing this speech. Conjure the emotion, then watch to see what body language and voice work develops from the feeling. Strive for three clear emotions. Review your recording and look for sharp emotional changes.

6.3.4 *Need for Super-Objective*

To know which emotions to shoot for, you need a clear super-objective. Find the purpose in the presentation, and you will know the right themes to use and the right tone and direction to go. Once determined, you can use emotional changes in a presentation to "reset" the audience's attention or to achieve proper pathos. One of the ways to ensure successful pathos is to sculpt your presentation with dynamic levels—break up the presentation into "beats."

An actor reads a script and decides when emotional changes are needed, depending on the words spoken. It tends to be at least every three to five minutes. You should do likewise. After writing a presentation with good logical flow, decide when emotional changes are needed. These are the beats within your presentation. Here is an excerpt from Patrick Henry's "Give me liberty, or give me death!" speech:

> This is no time for ceremony. The question before the House is one of awful moment to this country. For my own part, I consider it as nothing less than a question of freedom or slavery; and in proportion to the magnitude of the subject ought to be the freedom of the debate.

Here is the speech divided into beats, based on my own interpretation of the text. You may find a different emphasis for the speech by dividing the speech into different beats.

> This is no time for ceremony.

> The question before the House is one of awful moment to this country.

> For my own part, I consider it as nothing less than a question of freedom or slavery; and in proportion to the magnitude of the subject ought to be the freedom of the debate.

Here is the speech divided into beats, with emotional intentions assigned to each beat:

> This is no time for ceremony. [*Indignation*]

> The question before the House is one of awful moment to this country. [*Sadness*]

> For my own part, I consider it as nothing less than a question of freedom or slavery; and in proportion to the magnitude of the subject ought to be the freedom of the debate. [*Seriousness*]

Read this now. Perform it now as I have scored it with the indicated emotion and video or perform it with a friend or colleague. You will rate yourself below.

6.4 Score a Speech

Ever wonder how an actor runs to an audition, quickly scans a scene or monologue, and delivers a text with meaning and movement at first glance? Actors are taught how to score a text, and it can be a masterful tool for attorneys who are often short on time. An actor chooses something to focus on in a performance that helps him get into character: vocal speed, blocking, gestures, emotion, or facial expressions. The actor quickly makes notes on the text that reminds him to perform a certain way. Likewise, an attorney can make quick notes on a text to enhance voice, body language, emotion, or dynamics. I will show you how to score a presentation. I want you to read it and then perform and video it with a friend or colleague. Next I want you to finish scoring the Patrick Henry speech and then select a speech or presentation you've recently given and score it and then perform it. Remember a presentation could be the last pitch for a new client or an argument before a mediator or judge.

Score a Text Exercise

1. Beat divisions become a personal choice. I include divisions to "Eloquence of Daniel O'Connell" only as an example. You may divide this speech differently. Before you divide your beats, set a super-objective.

Eloquence of Daniel O'Connell

I do not think I exaggerate when I say that never since God made Demosthenes has he made a man better fitted for a great work than Daniel O'Connell. You may say that I am partial to my hero; but John Randolph of Roanoke, who hated an Irishman almost as much as he did a Yankee, when he got to London and heard O'Connell, the old slaveholder threw up his hands and exclaimed: "this is the man, those are the lips, the most eloquent that speak English in my day." And I think he was right.

Emerson says, "There is no true eloquence, unless there is a man behind the speech." Daniel O'Connell was listened to because all England and Ireland knew that there was a man behind the speech—one who could be neither bought, bullied, nor cheated.

And then, besides his irreproachable character, O'Connell had what is half the power of the popular orator; he had a majestic presence . . . . There was something majestic in his presence before he spoke, and he added to it the magnetism and grace that melts a million souls into his. When I saw him he was sixty-five—lithe as a boy, his every attitude a picture, his every gesture grace—he was still all nature; nothing but nature seemed to be speaking all over him. It would have been delicious to have watched him if he had not spoken a word, and all you thought of was a greyhound.

Then he had a voice that covered the gamut. I heard him once in Exeter Hall say, "I send my voice across

---

the Atlantic, careering like a thunderstorm against the breeze, to tell the slave-holder of the Carolinas that God's thunderbolts are hot, and to remind the bondman that the dawn of his redemption is already breaking." You seemed to hear his voice reverberating and re-echoing back to London from the Rocky Mountains. And then, with the slightest possible Irish brogue, he would tell a story that would make all Exeter Hall laugh, and the next moment tears in his voice, like an old song, and five thousand men wept. And all the while no effort—he seemed only breathing.

2. Divide the speech into beats, keeping your super-objective at the forefront of your mind.

> I do not think I exaggerate when I say that never since God made Demosthenes has he made a man better fitted for a great work than Daniel O'Connell.
>
> You may say that I am partial to my hero; but John Randolph of Roanoke, who hated an Irishman almost as much as he did a Yankee, when he got to London and heard O'Connell, the old slaveholder threw up his hands and exclaimed: "this is the man, those are the lips, the most eloquent that speak English in my day."
>
> And I think he was right.
>
> Emerson says, "There is no true eloquence, unless there is a man behind the speech." Daniel O'Connell was listened to because all England and Ireland knew that there was a man behind the speech—one who could be neither bought, bullied, nor cheated.
>
> And then, besides his irreproachable character, O'Connell had what is half the power of the popular orator; he had a majestic presence . . . . There was something majestic in his presence before he spoke, and he added to it the magnetism and grace that melts a million souls into his.
>
> When I saw him he was sixty-five—lithe as a boy, his every attitude a picture, his every gesture grace—he was still all nature; nothing but nature seemed to be speaking all over him.

It would have been delicious to have watched him if he had not spoken a word, and all you thought of was a greyhound.

Then he had a voice that covered the gamut. I heard him once in Exeter Hall say, "I send my voice across the Atlantic, careering like a thunderstorm against the breeze, to tell the slave-holder of the Carolinas that God's thunderbolts are hot, and to remind the bondman that the dawn of his redemption is already breaking."

You seemed to hear his voice reverberating and re-echoing back to London from the Rocky Mountains.

And then, with the slightest possible Irish brogue, he would tell a story that would make all Exeter Hall laugh,

and the next moment tears in his voice, like an old song, and five thousand men wept.

And all the while no effort—he seemed only breathing.

3. Pick emotional intentions for each beat.

[*Declarative*]

I do not think I exaggerate when I say that never since God made Demosthenes has he made a man better fitted for a great work than Daniel O'Connell.

[*Boisterous*]

You may say that I am partial to my hero; but John Randolph of Roanoke, who hated an Irishman almost as much as he did a Yankee, when he got to London and heard O'Connell, the old slaveholder threw up his hands and exclaimed: "this is the man, those are the lips, the most eloquent that speak English in my day."

[*Reflective*]

And I think he was right.

[*Sincere*]

Emerson says, "There is no true eloquence, unless there is a man behind the speech." Daniel O'Connell was listened to because all England and Ireland knew that there was a man behind the speech—one who could be neither bought, bullied, nor cheated.

[*Awe-Inspiring*]

And then, besides his irreproachable character, O'Connell had what is half the power of the popular orator; he had a majestic presence . . . . There was something majestic in his presence before he spoke, and he added to it the magnetism and grace that melts a million souls into his. When I saw him he was sixty-five—lithe as a boy, his every attitude a picture, his every gesture grace—he was still all nature; nothing but nature seemed to be speaking all over him.

[*Peaceful*]

It would have been delicious to have watched him if he had not spoken a word, and all you thought of was a greyhound.

[*Fervent*]

Then he had a voice that covered the gamut. I heard him once in Exeter Hall say, "I send my voice across the Atlantic, careering like a thunderstorm against the breeze, to tell the slave-holder of the Carolinas that God's thunderbolts are hot, and to remind the bondman that the dawn of his redemption is already breaking." You seemed to hear his voice reverberating and re-echoing back to London from the Rocky Mountains.

[*Lighthearted*]

And then, with the slightest possible Irish brogue, he would tell a story that would make all Exeter Hall laugh,

[*Tender*]

and the next moment tears in his voice, like an old song, and five thousand men wept. And all the while no effort—he seemed only breathing.

4. If you think the physical will inspire your interior, or you know you need more work on body language, try scoring the text with body language:

[Actor's neutral home base]

I do not think I exaggerate when I say that never since God made Demosthenes has he made a man better fitted for a great work than Daniel O'Connell.

[Gesture towards audience, walk forward, cup hands around mouth at quote]

You may say that I am partial to my hero; but John Randolph of Roanoke, who hated an Irishman almost as much as he did a Yankee, when he got to London and heard O'Connell, the old slaveholder threw up his hands and exclaimed: "this is the man, those are the lips, the most eloquent that speak English in my day."

[Return to neutral]

And I think he was right.

[Make eye contact with both sides of the audience]

Emerson says, "There is no true eloquence, unless there is a man behind the speech." Daniel O'Connell was listened to because all England and Ireland knew that there was a man behind the speech—one who could be neither bought, bullied, nor cheated.

[Erect posture, breathe deeply]

And then, besides his irreproachable character, O'Connell had what is half the power of the popular orator; he had a majestic presence . . . . There was something majestic in his presence before he spoke, and he added to it the magnetism and grace that melts a million souls into his.

[Facial expression looking to the right, remembering]

When I saw him he was sixty-five—lithe as a boy, his every attitude a picture, his every gesture grace—he was still all nature; nothing but nature seemed to be speaking all over him.

[Re-focus on audience]

It would have been delicious to have watched him if he had not spoken a word, and all you thought of was a greyhound.

[Big gestures, build to climax, beat fists together at end]

Then he had a voice that covered the gamut. I heard him once in Exeter Hall say, "I send my voice across the Atlantic, careering like a thunderstorm against the breeze, to tell the slave-holder of the Carolinas that God's thunderbolts are hot, and to remind the bondman that the dawn of his redemption is already breaking."

[Return to actor's neutral]

You seemed to hear his voice reverberating and re-echoing back to London from the Rocky Mountains.

[Find casual home base]

And then, with the slightest possible Irish brogue, he would tell a story that would make all Exeter Hall laugh, and the next moment tears in his voice, like an old song, and five thousand men wept.

[Inspiring facial expression]

And all the while no effort—he seemed only breathing.

5. If upward inflection troubles your speech pattern, you can score the text to identify operative words on which your voice should inflect. Simply bold or highlight the words in a text that you think need an upward stress in pitch.

> I do not think I **exaggerate** when I say that **never since God made Demosthenes** has he made a man better fitted for a great work than **Daniel** O'Connell.
>
> You **may** say that I am **partial** to my hero; but John Randolph of Roanoke, who **hated an Irishman** almost as **much** as he did a Yankee, when he got to London and **heard O'Connell**, the old slaveholder **threw up his hands** and exclaimed: "**this** is the man, **those** are the lips, the most **eloquent that speak English** in my day."
>
> And **I** think he **was right**.
>
> **Emerson** says, "There is **no true eloquence**, unless there is a **man** behind the speech." Daniel O'Connell was listened to because all England and Ireland knew that there was **a man behind the** speech—one who could be neither **bought, bullied**, nor cheated.

And then, besides his **irreproachable** character, O'Connell had what is **half the power** of the popular orator; he had a **majestic** presence . . . . There was something majestic in his presence **before he** spoke, and he added to it the **magnetism and grace** that **melts** a million souls into his.

When **I saw** him he was sixty-five—**lithe** as a boy, his every **attitude** a picture, his every **gesture** grace—he was still **all nature**; nothing but **nature** seemed to be speaking **all** over him.

It would have been **delicious** to have watched him if he had not **spoken** a word, and all you **thought of** was a greyhound.

Then he had a **voice** that covered the gamut. I heard him once in Exeter Hall say, "I **send my voice** across the Atlantic, **careering like** a thunderstorm against the breeze, to **tell the slave-holder** of the Carolinas that **God's thunderbolts** are hot, and to **remind the bondman** that the dawn of his redemption is **already** breaking."

You seemed to **hear** his voice reverberating and re-**echoing** back to London from the Rocky Mountains.

And then, with the slightest possible **Irish brogue**, he would tell a story that would make all Exeter Hall **laugh**, and the next moment **tears in his** voice, like an **old song**, and **five thousand** men wept.

And all the while no effort—he seemed **only** breathing.

6. If you are focused on speed changes, scoring a text with speed changes can help you advance the ball.

    [Increase speed through sentence]

    I do not think I exaggerate when I say that never since God made Demosthenes has he made a man better fitted for a great work than Daniel O'Connell.

    You may say that I am partial to my hero; [*PAUSE*] but John Randolph of Roanoke, who hated an Irishman almost as much as he did a Yankee, [*speed up*] when he got to London and heard O'Connell, the old slaveholder threw up his hands and exclaimed:

[*Slow and deliberate*]

"this is the man, those are the lips, the most eloquent that speak English in my day."

[*Return to normal pace*]

And I think he was right.

[*Even speed*]

Emerson says, "There is no true eloquence, unless there is a man behind the speech." Daniel O'Connell was listened to because all England and Ireland knew that there was a man behind the speech—one who could be neither bought, bullied, nor cheated.

And then, besides his irreproachable character, O'Connell had what is half the power of the popular orator; [*PAUSE*] he had a majestic presence . . . . [*PAUSE*] There was something majestic in his presence before he spoke, and he added to it the magnetism and grace that melts a million souls into his.

When I saw him he was sixty-five—lithe as a boy, his every attitude a picture, his every gesture grace—he was still all nature; [*PAUSE*] nothing but nature seemed to be speaking all over him.

[*Slow and even*]

It would have been delicious to have watched him if he had not spoken a word, and all you thought of was a greyhound.

[*Build momentum*]

Then he had a voice that covered the gamut. I heard him once in Exeter Hall say, "I send my voice across the Atlantic, careering like a thunderstorm against the breeze, to tell the slave-holder of the Carolinas that God's thunderbolts are hot, and to remind the bondman that the dawn of his redemption is already breaking." You seemed to hear his voice reverberating and re-echoing back to London from the Rocky Mountains.

And then, with the slightest possible Irish brogue, he would tell a story that would make all Exeter Hall laugh, [*PAUSE*] and the next moment tears in his voice, like an old song, and five thousand men wept. [*PAUSE*]

And all the while no effort—[*PAUSE*] he seemed only breathing.

7. Record yourself performing each style of scored text. Hold the paper high so you can read where and when you indicate a change. Review your performances and notice if a certain type of scoring helped you achieve a favorite reading of the passage. Remember that two qualified actors or attorneys can interpret a piece quite differently and have different results. You need to pick changes and direction that will achieve your super-objective.

Additional Scoring Exercise

1. Record yourself performing the following text (the Helen Keller speech you worked on earlier). After reviewing the performance, score the text. Pick one scoring method, and record yourself performing it. Review both performances and notice whether the scoring helped you achieve clearer emotion changes.

   To begin with, I have a word to say to my good friends, the editors, and others who are moved to pity me. Some people are grieved because they imagine I am in the hands of unscrupulous persons who lead me astray and persuade me to espouse unpopular causes and make me the mouthpiece of their propaganda. Now, let it be understood once and for all that I do not want their pity; I would not change places with one of them. I know what I am talking about. My sources of information are as good and reliable as anybody else's. I have papers and magazines from England, France, Germany and Austria that I can read myself. Not all the editors I have met can do that. Quite a number of them have to take their French and German second hand. No, I will not disparage the editors. They are an overworked, misunderstood class. Let them remember, though, that if I cannot see the fire at the end of their cigarettes, neither can they thread a needle in the dark. All I ask, gentle-

> men, is a fair field and no favor. I have entered the fight against preparedness and against the economic system under which we live. It is to be a fight to the finish, and I ask no quarter.

2. Record yourself performing your three-minute description of your practice (from chapter three). After reviewing the performance, score the text. Pick one scoring method, and record yourself performing your three-minute description of your practice. Review both performances and notice whether the scoring helped you achieve clearer emotion changes.

There is no wrong way to score. Clarifying your performance will make it better. You should be always moving toward your super-objective. Don't be afraid about not winning the Academy Award. Instead, avoid boring the audience. You will be more persuasive if you insert reasonable small doses of emotion into your presentations.

6.5 Learn to Memorize

Deliver the first couple minutes of a presentation without notes. There are techniques available to help you memorize large texts. Actors memorize hours of text for one-man shows. You can memorize more than you think.

Write the text so that it flows logically, as discussed in chapter three. Choose a super-objective, powerful themes, a clear format, and attend to the needs of the audience. Craft a buildup, climax, and resolution within the presentation. This breakdown will help jog your memory when you are delivering the text orally.

- Avoid trying to memorize long pieces. Instead, memorize transitions from one three-minute section to the next.

- Sing the speech—to avoid sounding mechanical after you memorize it, try singing the presentation, playing with vocal range, pauses, emphasis, and volume.

- Use refrains to help you memorize and bring back the main point.

- Plan specific gestures to trigger your memory at specific moments in the presentation.

CHAPTER SEVEN

SETTING GOALS AND STEPS TO IMPROVEMENT

*"Somewhere out there, he is training while I am not, and
when we meet, he will win."*

—Anonymous

The last six chapters have been full of theory, advice, exercises, and a lot of: "Do it this way." "Say that." "Stand here." "Move hands like this." "Show emotion." I targeted four areas in which improvement could enhance your oral presentation skills:

- preparing presentations;

- voice and speech pattern;

- body language; and

- emotion.

You should have a general sense of how you fared in each category. Your existing habits probably had much to do with how you did. Habits often have emotional underpinnings—certain nerves and fears condition you to slouch, clench your fists, or cast your eyes to the side. Some habits form out of ignorance. Habits develop over the years from many influences. Habits, like keeping hands closed or clenched, may also send inaccurate signals—irritation, nervousness, or anger. Changing a habit—often replacing one habit with another—takes courage, repetition, and time. To improve your skills, you need to periodically assess your skills, set realistic short-term and long-term goals, and then work on an improvement program, measuring progress and adjusting goals as necessary.

Most of the time, change usually happens with a gentle rain of hard work. If you try to forcibly alter you habits with a thunderbolt approach, you will most likely fail. Move the needle a little closer to improvement each day. With that said, I insist that short-term goals are necessary and achievable if you focus on the right ones and work. Here is a division of skills taught so far—grouped in the above categories of a successful presentation—and my recommended game plan for improvement.

Short-Term Goals	Long-Term Goals
Improve posture/carriage/dress	Improve breath support
Improve volume	Increase variety in speed/pauses
Solve vocal problems	Increase vocal range
Improve speech pattern	Improve eye contact
Connect emotionally	Add gestures
Move plot forward with gestures	Vary facial animation
Eliminate offensive attitudes and emotions	Eliminate nervous habits
Craft both thirty-second openings	Begin life-of-practice pitch deck
Craft three- to five-minute description	Learn impromptu recovery
Write clearly and concisely	

I have worked with attorneys who achieved their short-term goals with a few months of attention. This kind of improvement is possible on your own—without in-person coaching—if you will set goals and invest time and effort. You will need some sort of video-recording device and preferably a friend or colleague who can give you honest feedback. Immediate results, even acknowledgement of a bad habit, are important so you don't lose momentum, so let's stop for a moment, look at what you have learned, and re-set your goals.

The practice exercises have to be squeezed into busy schedules and are often uncomfortable to perform because they are unfamiliar—they are the things most people put off. You need to have a program to improve in those areas in which you are weak. For each category (preparing a presentation, voice and speech pattern, body language, and emotion), I provide a month (weekdays only) of daily exercises. I ask you to commit to twenty to thirty minutes of practice time each weekday. Except for "Preparing a Presentation," which I want you to do first, you can complete the other exercises in any order. By nailing well-crafted material, you have a platform to launch the stylistic changes in the other categories.

After completing the "Preparing a Presentation" month, choose your next month's work based on your weakest category—voice and speech pattern, body language, or emotion—and emphasize the areas of each category in which you are weakest. While you develop skills in the categories in which you are less proficient, rely on the strengths of your current oral communication style. For example, if you have fantastic body language but a weak voice, start a month of voice work after the month of preparation.

You are ready to attack your short-term goals. If we were working in person, I would give you homework, exercises, and other assignments to address the issues highlighted in your short-term goals. With the program I have laid out below, you can accomplish the same thing.

7.1 Preparing a Presentation—A Month of Change

Set aside thirty minutes a day to focus on writing new presentations and completing the writing exercises. Spend a few minutes each day identifying patterns in your practice—the recurring questions you are asked or problems you have to solve. Plan on devoting a total of thirty minutes a day on improving your preparation skills.

Preparing a Presentation—Week 1	
Day 1	1. Begin tracking common questions asked in your field so you can develop pre-packs. Write down these questions for future use. 2. Draft your thirty-second description for a sophisticated audience. Remember this description will be recycled and adapted for openings and introductions. 3. Before you leave the office for the evening, start the Skeletal Thinking Exercise.
Day 2	1. In the morning, complete the Skeletal Thinking Exercise. 2. Continue tracking common questions asked in your field so you can develop pre-packs. Write down these questions for future use. 3. Edit your thirty-second description for a sophisticated audience. 4. Before you leave the office for the evening, do the Skeletal Thinking Exercise.
Day 3	1. In the morning, complete the Skeletal Thinking Exercise. 2. Continue tracking common questions asked in your field so you can develop pre-packs. Write down these questions for future use. 3. Draft your thirty-second description for an unsophisticated audience. Remember this description will be recycled and adapted for openings and introductions. 4. Before you leave the office for the evening, do the Skeletal Thinking Exercise.

Preparing a Presentation—Week 1	
Day 4	1. In the morning, complete the Skeletal Thinking Exercise. 2. Continue tracking common questions asked in your field so you can develop pre-packs. Write down these questions for future use. 3. Edit your thirty-second description for an un-sophisticated audience. 4. Before you leave the office for the evening, do the Skeletal Thinking Exercise.
Day 5	1. In the morning, complete the Skeletal Thinking Exercise. 2. Continue tracking common questions asked in your field so you can develop pre-packs. Write down these questions for future use. 3. Record (only audio is necessary) yourself reading both thirty-second descriptions. Review the recordings and edit both thirty-second descriptions. 4. Before you leave the office for the evening, do the Skeletal Thinking Exercise.

Preparing a Presentation—Week 2	
Day 1	1. In the morning, complete the Skeletal Thinking Exercise. 2. Continue tracking common questions asked in your field so you can develop pre-packs. Write down these questions for future use. 3. Write five effective "I don't know" answers. 4. Before you leave the office for the evening, do the Skeletal Thinking Exercise.
Day 2	1. In the morning, complete the Skeletal Thinking Exercise. 2. Continue tracking common questions asked in your field so you can develop pre-packs. Write down these questions for future use. 3. Record (only audio is necessary) yourself reading both thirty-second descriptions. Review the recordings and edit both thirty-second descriptions. 4. Before you leave the office for the evening, do the Skeletal Thinking Exercise.

Preparing a Presentation—Week 2	
Day 3	1. In the morning, complete the Skeletal Thinking Exercise. 2. Continue tracking common questions asked in your field so you can develop pre-packs. Write down these questions for future use. 3. Record (only audio is necessary) yourself reading the five "I don't know" answers. Review the recording and edit as needed. 4. Before you leave the office for the evening, do the Skeletal Thinking Exercise.
Day 4	1. In the morning, complete the Skeletal Thinking Exercise. 2. Continue tracking common questions asked in your field so you can develop pre-packs. Write down these questions for future use. 3. Record (only audio is necessary) yourself reading both thirty-second descriptions. Review the recordings and edit both thirty-second descriptions. 4. Before you leave the office for the evening, do the Skeletal Thinking Exercise.
Day 5	1. In the morning, complete the Skeletal Thinking Exercise. 2. Continue tracking common questions asked in your field so you can develop pre-packs. Write down these questions for future use. 3. Record (only audio is necessary) yourself reading the five "I don't know" answers. Review the recording and edit as needed. Begin trying these "I don't know" answers in everyday situations, when questions arise to which you lack an appropriate response. 4. Before you leave the office for the evening, do the Skeletal Thinking Exercise.

Preparing a Presentation—Week 3	
Day 1	1. In the morning, complete the Skeletal Thinking Exercise. 2. Write a three- to five-minute description of yourself and your practice. 4. Before you leave the office for the evening, do the Skeletal Thinking Exercise.
Day 2	1. In the morning, complete the Skeletal Thinking Exercise. 2. Continue tracking common questions asked in your field so you can develop pre-packs. Write down these questions for future use. 3. Record (only audio is necessary) yourself reading both thirty-second descriptions. Review the recordings and edit both thirty-second descriptions. 4. Before you leave the office for the evening, do the Skeletal Thinking Exercise.
Day 3	1. In the morning, complete the Skeletal Thinking Exercise. 2. Continue tracking common questions asked in your field so you can develop pre-packs. Write down these questions for future use. 3. Record (only audio is necessary) yourself reading the three- to five-minute description. Review the recording and edit as needed. 4. Before you leave the office for the evening, do the Skeletal Thinking Exercise.
Day 4	1. In the morning, complete the Skeletal Thinking Exercise. 2. Continue tracking common questions asked in your field so you can develop pre-packs. Write down these questions for future use. 3. Record (only audio is necessary) yourself reading the three- to five-minute description. Review the recording and edit as needed. 4. Before you leave the office for the evening, do the Skeletal Thinking Exercise.

Preparing a Presentation—Week 3	
Day 5	1. In the morning, complete the Skeletal Thinking Exercise.
	2. Continue tracking common questions asked in your field so you can develop pre-packs. Write down these questions for future use.
	3. Record (only audio is necessary) yourself reading the three- to five-minute description. Review the recording and edit as needed.
	4. Before you leave the office for the evening, do the Skeletal Thinking Exercise.

Preparing a Presentation—Week 4	
Day 1	1. In the morning, complete the Skeletal Thinking Exercise.
	2. Draft three pre-packs, using the list compiled over the past three weeks of commonly asked questions.
	4. Before you leave the office for the evening, do the Skeletal Thinking Exercise.
Day 2	1. In the morning, complete the Skeletal Thinking Exercise.
	2. Record (only audio is necessary) yourself reading the three- to five-minute description of you and your practice. Review the recording and edit as needed.
	3. Before you leave the office for the evening, do the Skeletal Thinking Exercise.
Day 3	1. In the morning, complete the Skeletal Thinking Exercise.
	2. Record (only audio is necessary) yourself reading the pre-packs. Review the recording and edit as needed.
	3. Before you leave the office for the evening, do the Skeletal Thinking Exercise.
Day 4	1. In the morning, complete the Skeletal Thinking Exercise.
	2. Record (only audio is necessary) yourself reading the three- to five-minute description. Review the recording and edit as needed.
	3. Before you leave the office for the evening, do the Skeletal Thinking Exercise.

Preparing a Presentation—Week 4	
Day 5	1. In the morning, complete the Skeletal Thinking Exercise.
	2. Record (only audio is necessary) yourself reading both thirty-second descriptions, the three- to five-minute description of you and your practice, the five "I don't know" answers, and the pre-packs. Review the recordings and edit as needed.
	3. Continue developing additional pre-packs.

7.2   Voice and Speech Pattern—A Month of Change

You now have in your toolbox of prepared presentations the following material:

- thirty-second description/opening/introduction for a sophisticated audience;

- thirty-second description/opening/introduction for an unsophisticated audience;

- three- to five-minute description of you and your practice;

- "I don't know" answers; and

- three pre-packs.

Use this material to improve your voice and speech pattern. As your voice and speech pattern improves, continue refining the wording of this material.

Voice and Speech Pattern—Week 1	
Day 1	1. Pick one exercise for alignment, core strengthening, diaphragm, nerve control, and regulation. Perform these five exercises.
	2. On all phone calls during the day, focus on your posture and opening space for your diaphragm to expand and contract.
	3. On all phone calls during the day, project the volume of your voice through the ends of each sentence, avoiding any trailing-off problems.

Voice and Speech Pattern—Week 1	
Day 2	1. Pick one exercise for alignment, core strengthening, diaphragm, nerve control, and regulation. Perform these five exercises. 2. On all phone calls during the day, focus on your posture and opening space for your diaphragm to expand and contract. 3. On all phone calls during the day, record yourself with a smartphone or audio-recording device. Listen for overall speed problems. Adjust your overall speed (fast or slow) on all phone calls.
Day 3	1. Pick one exercise for alignment, core strengthening, diaphragm, nerve control, and regulation. Perform these five exercises. 2. On all phone calls during the day, focus on your posture and opening space for your diaphragm to expand and contract. 3. On all phone calls during the day, project the volume of your voice through the ends of each sentence and correct the overall speed of your speech.
Day 4	1. Pick one exercise for alignment, core strengthening, diaphragm, nerve control, and regulation. Perform these five exercises. 2. On all phone calls during the day, focus on your posture and opening space for your diaphragm to expand and contract. 3. On all phone calls during the day, project the volume of your voice through the ends of each sentence and correct the overall speed of your speech. 4. Record both thirty-second descriptions, focusing on volume and overall speed. Review the recordings and make changes as necessary.

Voice and Speech Pattern—Week 1	
Day 5	1. Pick one exercise for alignment, core strengthening, diaphragm, nerve control, and regulation. Perform these five exercises.
	2. On all phone calls during the day, focus on your posture and opening space for your diaphragm to expand and contract.
	3. On all phone calls during the day, project the volume of your voice through the ends of each sentence and correct the overall speed of your speech.
	4. Record both thirty-second descriptions, focusing on volume and overall speed. Review the recordings and make changes as necessary to volume and speed.

Voice and Speech Pattern—Week 2	
Day 1	1. Pick one exercise for alignment, core strengthening, diaphragm, nerve control, regulation, and articulation. Perform these six exercises.
	2. During all phone calls and meetings during the day, focus on your posture and opening space for your diaphragm to expand and contract.
	3. During all phone calls during the day and meetings, project the volume of your voice through the ends of each sentence and correct the overall speed of your speech.
Day 2	1. Pick one exercise for alignment, core strengthening, diaphragm, nerve control, regulation, and articulation. Perform these six exercises.
	2. During all phone calls and meetings during the day, focus on your posture and opening space for your diaphragm to expand and contract.
	3. During all phone calls and meetings during the day, project the volume of your voice through the ends of each sentence and correct the overall speed of your speech.
	4. Record the three- to five-minute description of you and your practice, focusing on volume and overall speed. Review the recording and make changes to volume and speed as necessary.

Voice and Speech Pattern—Week 2	
Day 3	1. Pick one exercise for alignment, core strengthening, diaphragm, nerve control, regulation, and articulation. Perform these six exercises. 2. During all phone calls and meetings during the day, focus on your posture and opening space for your diaphragm to expand and contract. 3. During all phone calls and meetings during the day, project the volume of your voice through the ends of each sentence and correct the overall speed of your speech. 4. Record the "I don't know" answers, focusing on volume and overall speed. Review the recordings and make changes to volume and speed as necessary.
Day 4	1. Pick one exercise for alignment, core strengthening, diaphragm, nerve control, regulation, and articulation. Perform these six exercises. 2. During all phone calls and meetings during the day, focus on your posture and opening space for your diaphragm to expand and contract. 3. During all phone calls and meetings during the day, project the volume of your voice through the ends of each sentence and correct the overall speed of your speech. 4. Record the pre-packs, focusing on volume and overall speed. Review the recordings and make changes to volume and speed as necessary.
Day 5	1. Pick one exercise for alignment, core strengthening, diaphragm, nerve control, regulation, and articulation. Perform these six exercises. 2. During all phone calls during the day, focus on your posture and opening space for your diaphragm to expand and contract. 3. During all phone calls during the day, project the volume of your voice through the ends of each sentence and correct the overall speed of your speech. 4. Record both thirty-second descriptions, focusing on volume and overall speed. Review the recordings and make changes to volume and speed as necessary.

Voice and Speech Pattern—Week 3	
Day 1	1. Pick one exercise for pitch, range, and inflection. Perform these three exercises. 2. On all phone calls during the day, focus on properly inflecting your voice downward in pitch at the ends of sentences. It may be necessary to make an audio recording of your performance on phone calls. Listen for an improper pattern of upward inflection at the ends of sentences. Correct upward inflection problems with the exercises on operative words.
Day 2	1. Pick one exercise for pitch, range, and inflection. Perform these three exercises. 2. On all phone calls during the day, focus on increasing the range of your voice used during a call. Try to use higher and lower notes than normal to expand your overall vocal range. It may be necessary to make an audio recording of your performance on phone calls. Listen to your current vocal range and expand it slightly on each call to accentuate important words or phrases.
Day 3	1. Pick one exercise for pitch, range, and inflection. Perform these three exercises. 2. On all phone calls during the day, focus on properly inflecting your voice downward in pitch at the ends of sentences. It may be necessary to make an audio recording of your performance on phone calls. Listen for an improper pattern of upward inflection at the ends of sentences. Correct upward inflection problems with the exercises on operative words.
Day 4	1. Pick one exercise for pitch, range, and inflection. Perform these three exercises. 2. On all phone calls during the day, focus on increasing the range of your voice used during a call. Try to use higher and lower notes than normal to expand your overall vocal range. It may be necessary to make an audio recording of your performance on phone calls. Listen to your current vocal range and expand it slightly on each call to accentuate important words or phrases.

Voice and Speech Pattern—Week 3	
Day 5	1. Pick one exercise for pitch, range, and inflection. Perform these three exercises.
	2. On all phone calls during the day, focus on properly inflecting your voice downward in pitch at the ends of sentences. It may be necessary to make an audio recording of your performance on phone calls. Listen for an improper pattern of upward inflection at the ends of sentences. Correct upward inflection problems with the exercises on operative words.

Voice and Speech Pattern—Week 4	
Day 1	1. Pick one exercise for pitch, range, and inflection. Perform these three exercises.
	2. During all phone calls and meetings during the day, focus on properly inflecting your voice downward in pitch at the ends of sentences. It may be necessary to make an audio recording of your performance on phone calls. Listen for an improper pattern of upward inflection at the ends of sentences. Correct upward inflection problems with the exercises on operative words.
Day 2	1. Pick one exercise for pitch, range, and inflection. Perform these three exercises.
	2. During all phone calls and meetings during the day, focus on increasing the range of your voice used during a call. Try to use higher and lower notes than normal to expand your overall vocal range. It may be necessary to make an audio recording of your performance on phone calls. Listen to your current vocal range and expand it slightly on each call to accentuate important words,or phrases.

Voice and Speech Pattern—Week 4	
Day 3	1. Pick one exercise for pitch, range, and inflection. Perform these three exercises. 2. During all phone calls and meetings during the day, focus on properly inflecting your voice downward in pitch at the ends of sentences. It may be necessary to make an audio recording of your performance on phone calls. Listen for an improper pattern of upward inflection at the ends of sentences. Correct upward inflection problems with the exercises on operative words. 3. On all phone calls today, add pauses to your speech pattern before any important point you wanted remembered by the audience.
Day 4	1. Pick one exercise for pitch, range, and inflection. Perform these three exercises. 2. During all phone calls and meetings during the day, focus on increasing the range of your voice used during a call. Try to use higher and lower notes than normal to expand your overall vocal range. It may be necessary to make an audio recording of your performance on phone calls. Listen to your current vocal range and expand it slightly on each call to accentuate important words or phrases. 3. On all phone calls today, add pauses to your speech pattern before any important point you wanted remembered by the audience.
Day 5	1. Pick one exercise for pitch, range, and inflection. Perform these three exercises. 2. During all phone calls and meetings during the day, focus on properly inflecting your voice downward in pitch at the ends of sentences. It may be necessary to make an audio recording of your performance on phone calls. Listen for an improper pattern of upward inflection at the ends of sentences. Correct upward inflection problems with the exercises on operative words. 3. During all phone calls and meetings today, add pauses to your speech pattern before any important point you wanted remembered by the audience.

7.3   Body Language — A Month of Change

As odd as it may seem, you should first practice body language changes during phone calls. Doing so allows you to experiment and make mistakes without any downside. I recommend turning off any video component on your phone during this exploration phase, so you don't give your caller an inadvertent comedy show.

Body Language—Week 1	
Day 1	1. Do the "Get Rid of the Worst" exercise. 2. Practice at least five different seated home bases during all phone calls. Transition between the home bases until you find a favorite three.
Day 2	1. Do the "Get Rid of the Worst" exercise. 2. Practice your three chosen, different seated home bases during all phone calls. Find times to transition from one to another.
Day 3	1. During all phone calls, maintain transitions between seated home bases. 2. In a seated position, practice adding exaggerated gestures every time you speak during a phone call.
Day 4	1. During all phone calls, maintain transitions between seated home bases. 2. In a seated position, practice including gestures while you speak, but minimize them to a normal intensity.
Day 5	1. During all phone calls, maintain transitions between seated home bases. 2. In a seated position, practice including gestures while you speak, but minimize them to a normal intensity. 3. In a seated position, do the "Divide the Space" exercise on every phone call during the day.

Body Language—Week 2	
Day 1	1. Do the "Get Rid of the Worst" exercise. 2. Practice at least five different standing home bases during all phone calls. Transition between the home bases until you find a favorite three.
Day 2	1. Do the "Get Rid of the Worst" exercise. 2. Practice your three chosen, different standing home bases during all phone calls. Find times to transition from one to another.
Day 3	1. During all phone calls, maintain transitions between seated home bases. 2. In a standing position, practice adding exaggerated gestures every time you speak during a phone call.
Day 4	1. During all phone calls, maintain transitions between seated home bases. 2. In a standing position, practice including gestures while you speak, but minimize them to a normal intensity.
Day 5	1. During all phone calls, maintain transitions between seated home bases. 2. In a standing position, practice including gestures while you speak, but minimize them to a normal intensity. 3. In a standing position, do the "Divide the Space" exercise on every phone call during the day.

	Body Language—Week 3
Day 1	1. Do the "Connection Exercise" during all phone calls, pretending that the audience is sitting across from you. 2. In a seated position, video-record yourself delivering both thirty-second descriptions, focusing on warm and engaging facial expressions throughout. Review the recordings and make appropriate adjustments.
Day 2	1. In a seated position, video-record yourself delivering your three- to five-minute description of you and your practice, focusing on warm and engaging facial expressions. Review the recordings and make appropriate adjustments.
Day 3	1. In a seated position, video-record yourself delivering your three- to five-minute description of you and your practice, focusing on warm and engaging facial expressions and specific gestures that help the audience understand your message. Review the recordings and make appropriate adjustments.
Day 4	1. In a seated position, video-record yourself delivering your three- to five-minute description of you and your practice, focusing on warm and engaging facial expressions, specific gestures that help the audience understand your message, and transitioning between home bases. Review the recordings and make appropriate adjustments.
Day 5	1. In a standing position, video-record yourself delivering your three- to five-minute description of you and your practice, focusing on warm and engaging facial expressions, specific gestures that help the audience understand your message, and transitioning between home bases. Review the recordings and make appropriate adjustments.

Body Language—Week 4	
Day 1	1. On all phone calls, practice using a prop in your hand, noting pitfalls to avoid. 2. During all meetings, practice keeping good alignment and strong posture.
Day 2	1. During all small meetings, make eye contact with each audience member. 2. Practice keeping proper posture in all meetings. 3. During all meetings, practice including gestures while you speak, but minimize them to a normal intensity.
Day 3	1. During all small meetings, make eye contact with each audience member. 2. Practice keeping proper posture in all meetings. 3. During all meetings, practice including gestures while you speak, but minimize them to a normal intensity.
Day 4	1. During all meetings, practice transitioning between seated home bases. 2. During all meetings, practice including gestures while you speak, but minimize them to a normal intensity. 3. During all meetings, practice the "Divide the Space" exercise.
Day 5	1. During all meetings, practice transitioning between seated home bases. 2. During all meetings, practice including gestures while you speak, but minimize them to a normal intensity. 3. During all meetings, practice warm and engaging facial expressions during opening and closing remarks, where appropriate.

7.4 Emotion—A Month of Change

The number of action items for "Emotion—Weeks 2–4" is slim. This is because the exercises take more time.

Emotion—Week 1	
Day 1	1. On all phone calls, increase your "small talk" time with audience members. 2. Begin tracking times during the day when you become exceedingly nervous during an oral communication. Keep a record of these times, noting whether they are during planned presentations or impromptu situations, whether they happen with large or small audiences.
Day 2	1. On all phone calls, increase your "small talk" time with audience members. 2. Continue tracking times during the day when you become exceedingly nervous during an oral communication. Keep a record of these times, noting whether they are during planned presentations or impromptu situations, whether they happen with large or small audiences. 3. Begin controlling the surge of anxiety of nervous moments with flex and release exercises.
Day 3	1. On all phone calls, increase your "small talk" time with audience members. 2. Continue tracking times during the day when you become exceedingly nervous during an oral communication. Keep a record of these times, noting whether they are during planned presentations or impromptu situations, whether they happen with large or small audiences. 3. Begin controlling the surge of anxiety of nervous moments with flex and release exercises. 4. With an eye towards "dressing the part," take inventory of your wardrobe and ensure you have professional attire and grooming items. If not, fill those gaps.

Emotion—Week 1	
Day 4	1. Arrive at each meeting with a spirit of enthusiasm and energy. 2. Do the "Outside-In" exercise.
Day 5	1. Practice small talk at every meeting. 2. Perform the "Outside-In" exercise using your three- to five-minute description of you and your practice.

Emotion—Week 2	
Day 1	1. Do the "Inside-out" exercise.
Day 2	1. Do the "Inside-out" exercise using your three- to five-minute description of you and your practice.
Day 3	1. Do the "Score a Text" exercise, focusing on Emotion Intentions and Body Language.
Day 4	1. Do the "Score a Text" exercise, focusing on Facial Expressions and Speed Changes.
Day 5	1. Do the "Score a Text" exercise, using your three- to five-minute description of you and your practice. Focus on Emotion Intentions and Body Language.

Emotion—Week 3	
Day 1	1. Do the "Score a Text" exercise, using your three- to five-minute description of you and your practice. Focus on Facial Expression and Body Language.
Day 2	1. On each phone call, deliver three different subtle emotions at specific times—e.g., warmth, determination, confidence.
Day 3	1. During each phone call and meeting, deliver three different subtle emotions at specific times— e.g., warmth, determination, confidence.
Day 4	1. Memorize the thirty-second description for a sophisticated audience.
Day 5	1. Memorize the thirty-second description for an unsophisticated audience.

Emotion—Week 4	
Day 1	1. Memorize the pre-packs.
Day 2	1. Memorize the "I don't know" answers.
Day 3	1. Memorize the three- to five-minute description of you and your practice.
Day 4	1. Record a performance of both thirty-second descriptions, focusing on three distinct emotional changes within each performance. Review the performances and make needed adjustments.
Day 5	1. Record a performance of the three- to five-minute description of you and your practice, focusing on three distinct emotional changes within the performance. Review the performances and make needed adjustments.

CHAPTER EIGHT

NONLITIGATOR TRACK

"To improve is to change; to be perfect is to change often."

—Winston Churchill

The divide between the litigator and nonlitigator tracks is narrow when discussing rhetoric skills. The challenges and solutions in oral communications are more alike than different. That being said, this chapter provides tips primarily for the nonlitigator.

Nonlitigators need to perform just like litigators. There is a misconception that litigators only use oral presentation skills when they are on stage in the courtroom or at a deposition. Not true. Lawyers need to persuade in all settings. Litigators and nonlitigators are on stage in conference rooms, telephone conference calls, and negotiation sessions. These may be "off-Broadway" performances, but they are just as critical to a successful career and used far more often. Lawyers are performing all the time—whether they are meeting with and organizing their team to move forward with an M&A transaction or litigation, closing a real estate deal, debating legislation, negotiating a contract, or arguing a motion in a courtroom.

In this chapter, I cover telephone calls, meetings, tips from lobbyists applicable for all lawyers, business development, and strategies for working in groups. While I cover them separately, it's not that simple in real practice. Matters can last a long time, with the members and relationships on each side of the matter evolving throughout the representation. Lawyers play a team sport most days—at larger firms especially, matters are "bigger" and it's like a group event. Someone manages a contact list. A team represents the client; your firm may be lead counsel, but there could be local or specialized counsel; there could be an investment banking firm involved and possibly some financial or other expert and they have members of their teams. Your firm puts together its team. There's a partner in charge of a younger partner and some associates, but your firm's team has a few subteams with real estate or other specialties. The other side of the matter may be similarly staffed. So when I talk about a phone call, meeting, or conference call, it is not that simple.

The playing field for oral communication is mixed now that business is busy, global, and diverse. Rarely will you have a one-time phone call in isolation. Handling a matter or deal means hundreds of calls and meetings with various parties inside and outside the law. I segregate the topics within this chapter, recognizing that real legal practice is a hybrid of venues—a mix of telephone calls, videoconferencing, and meetings with one or many present in a room together. Tips for one section of this chapter naturally apply to others, since a conference call might happen during a meeting.

8.1 Mastering a Phone Call

The bad news is that many attorneys live on the phone, and an attorney who is unable to instill confidence and persuade over the telephone is in danger of failing. The good news is that the telephone provides physical anonymity, allowing you to focus on improvements in only three elements of style: voice and speech pattern, emotion and dynamics, and, of course, preparation of the presentation. Unless it's a videoconference, you can set aside body language because your voice reigns in this scenario. To succeed on a call, you must not forget Aristotle and keep in mind that the art of persuasion requires ethos (good character), pathos (emotion), and logos (reason). You must also remember that we persuade best with simple, logical and powerful speech—even on the phone. As we talk about these off-Broadway shows— phone and conference calls, meetings, interviews, lobbying, etc.—remember that you may present in different roles. You will structure your preparation and presentation to serve your effort—achieve a super-objective—in your specific role at the time. You could lead a call or just be on the call to provide some background or expertise in one area; you could be a member of a team making a pitch to a new client or managing a major piece of a deal.

How do certain attorneys control a call or participate effectively? Why are certain attorneys and their argument or presentation remembered after a conference call? Sure, some lawyers are naturally confident, clear, and compelling and possess some raw talent; they have 1) a knack for clear and concise messaging, 2) a good voice (not perfect in quality, but pleasing to hear), and 3) average emotional expression. Even if you lack this raw talent, you can nevertheless improve significantly by focusing on the compensation techniques illustrated within the exercises in this book.

The two most frequent complaints I hear regarding someone's inadequacy on a telephone call are 1) she doesn't know when to jump in, or 2) he speaks too much. Preparing properly for the call helps solve both problems. Determine ahead of time your role and reason for being on the call. You must know this to develop a super-objective and the themes that will help you achieve it.

If you are leading the call, try to let each person on the call know, clearly and specifically, why that person is included—to the extent possible, of course. If a young associate is invited to join a conference call, let him know whether he is expected to listen and learn or handle a discreet matter. At the opening of the call, kick off with small talk that helps the parties get to know another and build relationships. In case some conference members are late dialing in, think of ways to chat with each member to fill the time until everyone chimes in—and, of course, do this before the call begins, so you're not scrambling to fill the void. Ask about their family. Talk about their recent tennis match. Find out where they will go on vacation. Think about ways to connect personally, even if you are on opposite sides of a matter. Matters can last a long time in the life of a practice, so relationship building helps you maintain the trust of clients and parties. Negotiations go farther when the other side genuinely likes you. If you want someone's attention on a personal or business topic that you know interests the person, ask a question and listen. That person will think you are a good conversationalist. It doesn't take much to get a person's interest. When you walk into a room, look for pictures or desk paraphernalia that give a lead. You can never go wrong by complimenting the cute kids or dog on the screensaver or to ask about sailing or fishing if evidence of those interest clutters the office.

If you are a member of the call but not a key player, find a brief way to show your purpose on the call. At the beginning of the matter, it matters most—the first impression sticks. Knowing something about the team is easy today with the internet, and a background search helps you prepare for that first opportunity to introduce yourself. If the opportunity arises, deliver a crisp, fifteen- to thirty-second prepared introduction of yourself that explains your useful specialty. Be sure to project your voice and evenly space your speech pattern. Figure out ahead of time why you are on the call and set a clear super-objective, possibly even map out a few strong themes in advance. If you misunderstand or fail to ascertain your purpose, you run the risk of staying silent or jumping in out of turn. As an auxiliary member of a call, you might not be remembered for your silent presence, but you should make appropriate efforts to connect through casual conversation during breaks. Also, your well-prepared introduction can establish the right ethos and pathos.

Defining your purpose and goal for a call also prevents long-winded discussions. Create an organized outline before a call to delineate exactly what you need to communicate (preparation of the presentation). Unless you are asked a tangential question, stay on point. Stick to your outline, and respect the time of each audience member. If you have to speak for an extended period of time, consider providing visual aids or an agenda in advance to help move the call along in an organized fashion. Also consider 1) breaking up a monologue into smaller segments, separated by a short question-and-answer period, or 2) dividing the substance between colleagues to reset the audience's attention. Remember the three-minute rule of thumb—the need to reset an audience's attention—we talked about in chapter three. An audience can fall asleep or drift away on a phone call, too.

You deliver good oral presentation by using simple, logical, and powerful speech. Powerful does not mean loud. A powerful voice is one that is heard and carries force even through a whisper. Telephones can be tricky. Staying sensitive to equipment malfunctions can save your effectiveness. If you have the decision-making power and the funds, invest in the right equipment to transmit clear sound to your audience on a call. A hands-free headset provides lower white-noise interruption than a speaker phone. By being mindful of the quality of the equipment, you can prevent the listener by suffering undue frustration. If you have never taken the time to test how your phone system sounds on speaker or conference or when connected to a global call, have a test run and address any problems so your voice can shine. If you are taking a call alone from your office, don't go on speaker if you have to present. On the telephone, your voice delivers everything. Attorneys often go on the speaker not to be hands-free to take notes, but to do something else on their computers while the call evolves. If the call matters, pick up the handset and avoid the risk of bad resonance or static.

A bad connection can cause delays, requiring you to speak with more pauses and listen for interruptions from other members of the call. Multiple connections cause interruption confusion unless a call leader is identified. As the leader of a conference call, request that all those on cell phones push the "mute" button to provide clearer sound transmission. On a conference call, position yourself near the telephone or conference device to more easily direct your voice with the right amount of force, impacting the power and the quality of your voice to those other participants on the call. Below is an exercise to practice the force variation and voice control necessary for successful conference calls. Each text, due to its content, requires you to increase intensity

---

Force Variation Exercise

Take a few minutes now to practice reading the texts provided below, remembering the voice and speech pattern lessons from chapter four.

Most of us are reluctant to read out loud. Someone could walk by the office and look in and see us talking to ourselves. Close the door and read these texts aloud.

1. The context of words necessitates certain levels of volume and word stress, which I refer to as "force." In this first reading, the poet hears a distant bugle in the background. Speak the text with a gentle force—medium volume, drawing out words so vowel sounds sound fluid and long. Imagine connecting with an old friend with this tone over the phone.

   [*Gentle*]

   Hark, O hear! How thin and clear,

   And thinner, clearer, farther going;

---

sweet and far, from cliff and scar,

The horns of Elfland faintly blowing.[1]

2. The next text by Emerson comprises "words of wisdom." The force should be moderate, with a full volume and even emphasis on each word, plotting pauses at natural breaks in the text (commas, periods). This tone would be correct for advising a client on a matter over the phone. No anger or tension in the voice.

[*Moderate*]

Once or twice in a lifetime we are permitted to enjoy the charm of noble manners, in the presence of men or women who have no bar in their nature, but whose character emanates freely in their word and gesture.

A beautiful form is better than a beautiful face; a beautiful behavior is better than a beautiful form: it gives a higher pleasure than statues or pictures, —it is the finest of the fine arts.[2]

3. The final text demands a stronger force—higher volume and crisper speed. You can sense the excitement in the words, and your voice should reflect it. This tone can be easily used when tensions run high over the phone and you need to motivate or correct another party.

[*Strong*]

As the line halted Napoleon shouted to the drummer-boy, "Beat a retreat!" The boy stepped forward, grasped his drumsticks and said," Sire, I do not know how. I have never been taught that. But I can beat a charge. Oh! I can beat a charge that will make the very dead fall into line . . . ."[3]

One last point: know who and where the audience is. Not only should you research the participants on the call to know how to craft your super-objective and themes, but you need to understand where they are physically located. For example, if the president of your client is taking a call from his car while driving with his

---

1. Lord Alfred Tennyson, "Blow, Bugle, Blow."
2. Ralph Waldo Emerson, Essay 16, "Manners."
3. Charles Alphonso Smith, Lida Brown McMurry, The Smith-McMurry Language Series (Google Books).

family to the beach, it may not be the best time for too much data, details, or decisions. Adjust that agenda and super-objective.

8.1.1 Webinars

If you are speaking via webinar, ask the coordinator if the participants will see your slides only or a combination of slides and video. Add commentary to each slide in a deck—don't simply read the slide to the audience. The webinar participants join the webinar to hear your insights, not to have slides read to them.

8.1.2 Group Conference Calls

If you join a conference call in a conference room with other participants, direct your volume toward the device, but keep connected to the people in the room with you by making eye contact occasionally, gesturing towards them, and maintaining your professional poise. If the person you want to convince is in the conference room, speak directly to that individual and let the device pick up the necessary sound for the remote audience members.

8.2 Mastering a Meeting

A face-to-face meeting adds the element of body language. Mastering the body language for a meeting usually means honing your seated home bases,[4] eye contact, gestures, and overall energy. A recent study[5] about the most annoying body language during interviews highlights the physical behaviors to avoid in meetings:

- failure to make appropriate eye contact;
- lack of smile;
- fidgeting too much;
- bad posture;
- crossing arms over chest;
- playing with hair or touching the face; and
- using too many hand gestures.

This study confirms what we covered in chapter five about useful body language in a meeting: make eye contact, smile, stop fidgeting, correct posture, and add gestures suitable and natural for the space and audience. Maintaining good eye contact is often more difficult in a meeting in a conference room than in a presentation in a conference hall. In the conference room, eye contact is more direct and harder to share than it is when a speaker gazes from a podium in the general direction of

---

4. *See* chapter five.
5. "What not to do in the interview," Careerbuilder.com, at https://www.careerbuilder.com/advice/what-not-to-do-in-the-interview.

segments of the audience. Speaking roles and rank generally determine where you sit in a conference room. If you lead the meeting, sit in a position that allows you to "direct traffic," transitioning between speakers or initiating question and answer periods. If you sit at a round table, the positions are naturally equalized. If at a rectangular table, allow the speaker or ranking member of a group to sit at the head of the table or in the center of the long side of the table.

Whether you are on a conference call or in a meeting or some combination, recognize that there are different audiences. You need to address the key person or persons in the audience without diminishing the others. The others may be members of your firm or team. Address and include them with eye contact, body language, and verbal interaction during the presentation since they are part of the key audience. Don't leave them out or showboat. Knowing who the key audience is and focusing on him without pandering is difficult. Addressing the key audience includes fashioning the presentation to build ethos, pathos, and logos with them. But if you ignore other members of a meeting, you hurt your ultimate chances of success. Discussions might happen in private, and you don't want to offend someone in the meeting by failing to connect with them through eye contact, body positioning, and directed gestures.

When you lead a meeting, you must control the room. This presents challenges when personalities are big. The following are some tips for leading an effective meeting.

- Keep the meeting on track; let it flow, but always return to the point.

- Station yourself at the head or in the middle of the table; remember to maintain eye contact with the key participant.

- Lead by example; use your super-objective to set the tone for the meeting.

- Think about the meeting structure. During the planning phase, determine whether to hold a structured or unstructured meeting. Once you have decided, be sure to tell the participants so they can prepare accordingly (e.g., a PowerPoint presentation, etc.).

- Play to the strengths of your team members and work proactively through the weaknesses by bringing out the best in people. For example, John is brilliant, but a terrible communicator. Don't ask him to elaborate unnecessarily; avoid open-ended questions. Also, women generally perform worse than their male counterparts in meetings; find ways to facilitate value-adding contributions from your female colleagues on the team. In 2012, the American Political Science Review published a study out of Brigham Young University and Princeton University that found women speak 25 percent less than their male counterparts.[6] The study also found that when a group worked from consensus, women were more likely to speak up. A great way to encourage participation is to make specific assignments and explain your expectations to those in your control ahead of time.

- At any meeting, but especially when you meet with your team and the other side, be mindful that the other side will notice how you treat your team members. Many attorneys tell me that they felt their firm failed to win a new client following a beauty-contest presentation because the client said the firm's team didn't seem to be cohesive and the elements of style—body language, voice, emotion—just didn't seem right among the members off the team. Remember, it's a team sport.

If you are asked to run a meeting, take the time to prepare, incorporating the oral communication skills and leadership tips you learn from respected colleagues. Be a sponge of best practices.

You will not always be the leader of a meeting. There are more roles in a meeting to be examined—silent observers and those required to listen and respond to a presentation. How should they behave in a meeting? How can they achieve ethos, pathos, and logos when meetings are called? Below is a table of meeting roles and corresponding tips in each of the four major categories of oral communication: preparation, voice and speech pattern, body language, and emotion. Use these strategies to fulfill any role in a meeting.

Tips for the Meeting Organizer	
Presentation	• Prepare with a super-objective and themes that fit the audience.
	• Outline the meeting, with time divisions.
	• Assign roles to the members of your team who will be at the meeting and make sure they prepare for their presentations
	• Assign appropriate pieces of the presentation to necessary parties.
	• Create and synch handouts and visual aids.
	• Send materials ahead of time for review, including agendas and logistical information.
	• Arrange for all meeting room logistics.

---

6. KARPOWITZ, CHRISTOPHER F., TALI MENDELBERG, and LEE SHAKER. "Gender Inequality in Deliberative Participation." The American Political Science Review 106, no. 3 (2012): 533-47. http://www.jstor.org/stable/23275432.

Tips for the Meeting Organizer	
Voice and Speech Pattern	• Project your voice slightly more than you think necessary. • Enunciate. • Slow down. • Avoid upward inflection.
Body Language	• Enter the room with facial expressions appropriate for the tone of the meeting. • Align posture. • Sit at a place in the room where the key member of the audience members can see and hear you. • Make eye contact with everyone in the room during the first two minutes of your opening. Then focus primarily on the decision-makers in the room. • Position your body (gestures and directionality) toward the decision-makers in the room, but do not ignore the others present. • If a question is asked, maintain eye contact with the person asking the question, knowing that sometimes the person you want to hear the answer is another person. Keep eye contact and body language directed there for the first few moments of your answer, then open up your physicality—eye contact and body language—to the whole group to tie back the applicability of your answer to the whole group.
Emotion	• Your super-objective should set the tone. • Greet everyone respectfully, and if appropriate, with friendliness and warmth. Allow for more time if it's a first-time meeting. • Make it a point to find specific times in the presentation to vary emotion.

Tips for a Meeting Presenter	
Presentation	• Predict presentation content and outline potential responses. • Coordinate shifting among other members of your team. • If varying responses exist, create a decision tree with bullet points under each potential response. • Create and rehearse a thirty-second introduction in case you are asked to introduce your self. • Research meeting participants. • Read any materials sent by the participants. • Dress professionally.
Voice and Speech Pattern	• Project voice. • Use few words (avoid the temptation to become long-winded when asked for a response). • Slow down. • Avoid upward inflection.
Body Language	• Sit in a dominant place in the room. • Maintain eye contact when possible with the audience. • Take notes sparingly. • Track questions, if needed. • Keep posture energized and engaged. • Avoid fidgeting.
Emotion	• Patiently listen to the presentation. • Control reactions that might weaken your position. • Once you perceive the tone of the presentation, return an appropriate tone.

Tips for a Meeting Participant	
Presentation	• Clarify before the meeting why your attendance is needed.
	• Clarify your responsibilities at the meeting.
	• Create and rehearse a thirty-second introduction in case you are asked to introduce your self.
	• Research meeting participants.
	• Read any materials sent by the other participants.
	• Dress professionally, not flashy, and preferably one level dressier than your host. This shows respect for the event and leaves a powerful first impression of professionalism.
	• Think of potential value-added commentary for the meeting and prepare specific points to offer when asked.
	• Observe the meeting with a critical eye, looking for reactions from the audience, and be able to give valuable feedback if asked at breaks or at the end.
Voice and Speech Pattern	• Project voice.
	• Keep introduction to thirty seconds or less.
	• Slow down.
	• Avoid upward inflection.
Body Language	• Greet meeting participants with a friendly facial expression and firm handshake. You may only have this one moment to connect with this participant and/or speak.
	• Correct posture, both sitting and standing.
	• Avoid using laptops (they hide your face and make you appear secretarial).
	• Follow body language cues from ranking members of the meeting.
Emotion	• Portray friendliness, confidence, and interest.

8.3   Business Development

The single most important tool for business development is great oral communication skills. It's the face-to-face with the potential client (or when she heard while you were representing someone else) that clinches the representation. Entire consulting firms exist to develop business for attorneys. Firms have comprehensive business development plans and usually ask each attorney to develop his or her own. Firms produce fancy brochures and polished slides that list clients, values, experience, and bios. You've seen them, prepared them, and used them. But if you don't "wow" a potential client when you open your mouth, you will probably not grow your legal practice. Whether you practice in the government or private practice, lawyers serve clients. Attorneys need good client-service communication skills to succeed.

The materials presented throughout this book (e.g., thirty-second descriptions, three- to five-minute description, lifetime-practice pitch deck, pre-packs) help develop your reputation and highlight your specialization. To further the quality of the material, collaborate with your marketing department or human resources department to be in concert with the branding messages for you as well as your firm or department.

Preparing and delivering a polished pitch is essential. Pitches can be casual (dinner or golf) or formal (board room—seated or standing presentation). Here are some basic tips for pitch preparation.

8.3.1 Craft the Presentation Using Confident and Powerful Language

Don't apologize for not being like your competition. Use inclusive language choices, such as "we" instead of "you." Describe yourself with bold terms, highlighting successes and finding a way to make lemonade out of any lemons.

8.3.2 Research the Client's Needs and Address Them

I bet most potential clients fan through marketing materials. However, they meet with you in person to start a conversation and to measure you. So have one. Listen and respond directly and openly to their needs.

8.3.3 Show Your Problem-Solving Skills in the Pitch

Offer a menu of solutions to a new client once you ascertain a concern. Some attorneys fear giving away information or advice for free, but a kernel of advice goes a long way and showcases your creative potential.

8.3.4 Create Simple, Effective Graphics

Or don't bring any. A new client is not there to see a laser light show. The client does not want to squint at a screen with too many words. Use visual aids that do not detract from you. After the presentation, you can give the prospective client a take-away book of information.

8.3.5 *Offer Options, Give Advice, and Be Flexible*

You can offer a menu of options and give the client the path you would recommend. If the client disagrees, stay flexible and be willing to help her achieve her goal in another way. Since you don't have all the information or total perspective, be prepared to change directions as necessary.

8.3.6 *Plan and Practice*

Whether you deliver a pitch solo or with a team of attorneys, plan and practice. If you give a pitch alone, you need to entertain the audience for a long period of time. This takes practice and creativity to avoid monotony. If you deliver a pitch with a group, take care to organize your team's delivery and avoid duplicating material. Remember that how you relate and interact with members of your team can have an impact on a potential client's decision.

8.3.7 *Create a Template to Recycle*

When pitch opportunities arise, spend your time researching the client and practicing your presentation skills. The potential client wants to hear about solutions you have for her. Descriptions of you should relate directly with the strategies and services you could offer.

If it is a group presentation, have the group practice together. To open time for that work, have ready a template or "pitch book"—recyclable information about your experience and the services you provide. This pitch book in not something you hand to a client. It serves as a preparation tool for you. A pitch book should have 1) your personal description; 2) clear, consistent, and scripted talking points about your firm; 3) clear, consistent, and scripted talking points about your specialty; 4) examples of your representations in the past; and 5) adaptable visual aid templates that help you describe your experience. Items 1 through 4 should be pre-packs[7] that you have down cold.

8.3.8 *Know How to Cross-Sell within Your Firm*

Research where and how practice groups intersect so you can achieve a wider representation or score a piece of ancillary business. Often, a question and answer period dovetails into discovering additional legal needs of the client. Rehearse pitches with attorneys from other practice groups or departments to properly describe the nexus between the practice groups and brainstorm ways to expand legal services for the client.

---

7. *See* chapter three.

8.4 Lobbying Lessons

There is a group of attorneys who capitalize on oral communication to sway their audiences on a daily basis. Lobbying lawyers attempt to influence government officials at every level of government. Lobbyists are in high demand because of increasingly regulated industries. The ever-encroaching government means that every business and nonprofit is directly affected by decisions made by government officials who carry out governing regulations. Lobbyists have their work cut out for them.

This elite group of communicators has lessons to share about presentation, networking, media usage, and negotiation. All attorneys can benefit from their after-action reports and battle scars.

8.4.1 Establish Yourself as an Expert in a Field

Seek opportunities to showcase your expertise through forward-thinking mediums. Today, clients want deep expertise from a well-known source. Embrace social media and become savvy in the wide variety of media the digital age.

8.4.2 Make Every Contact Important

Every interaction during the day is an opportunity to establish credibility and build your personal brand. The college summer intern may turn out to be your biggest client ten years from now—so cultivate relationships.

8.4.3 Be Smart with the Media

Reporters have control of a written quote or a video cut. Establishing a network of reporters with whom you share professional courtesies to review quotes before publication avoids embarrassing media coverage. Even if a relationship is established, always assume every comment is "on the record." When interacting with the media, your goals should be to make yourself likable and reliable. Keep facts straight and do not over-promise. If you are asked to represent your firm, brush up on current projects, particularly if they are showcased on the firm website. Decide on your communication objectives and find a way to weave them into your answers. One way to prepare for a journalist interview is to research the audience for whom the journalist writes. Are they biased? Do they have a known agenda?

8.4.4 Learn to Handle the Negative

If you are handling a sensitive topic or delivering bad news to a client or colleague, practice dealing with the negativity and ending an answer with a positive perspective.

8.4.5 Use Fewer Words

Sometimes a lobbyist is given only five minutes with a government official, so her message musts must be laser tight. Be concise, target answers for a specific audience, and craft the answers to the audience's understanding of the situation.

8.4.6 Ask for Questions

Consider asking for a list of questions before you meet with an important client or colleague—explain that you are doing so to make efficient use of time. Even if the audience asks you an additional, unexpected question, you can properly prepare for the unexpected with an initial insight into the prepared questions.

8.4.7 Learn What Not to Do

Lobbyists learn quickly what not to do. Frank Vlossak, partner at Williams Jensen, a lobbying law firm in Washington DC, provided a list of best practices that work well even when not dealing with a member of Congress. While these are created within the world of lobbying, the principles apply to every legal practice.

Best Practices or What Not to Do

- *Always be respectful of the Senator's/Member's/staffer's time.* Be on time for your meeting. Be concise and allow time for questions. Encourage your client to do the same. Request meetings well in advance. Do not ask for a meeting the day before and expect to get one. In any legal practice, respect the audience's time by arriving promptly and keeping the message efficient. Having a clear super-objective and a few well-crafted themes will help you manage time. You lose your point when the audience starts looking at watches or playing with devices.

- *Prepare your client.* Give your clients your best counsel on how to handle a meeting, but defer to them based on their preferences. Some clients like to do all the talking, which they can and should do if they prefer to play that role. Preparing your client includes logistics: congressional schedules are unpredictable. Your appointment with a Member or Senator may be cancelled at the last minute or taken by staff. You may be escorted to the offices adjoining a hearing room where the Member or Senator is participating in committee business. Also make your client understand that the energy level, mood, and engagement of the people you are meeting will vary. This is (almost always) a function of the day the person you are meeting with has had. Clients should not take it personally if a Senator or staffer seems distracted or tired, particularly at the end of a long day or during a busy congressional work period. Many attorneys have war stories of clients that crumble because you failed to prepare them properly.

- *Research your audience.* It is vitally important to know who you are meeting, including their positions on the subject matter of the appointment. While your client's message should be consistent in all contacts, how you present your issue will depend on the elected official's voting history, level of interest in the subject, committee assignments, and career before being elected to Congress. Careful research in preparation for a client executive's visit with a Member of Congress may turn up things they have in common or other topics that can make the initial conversation more personal and pleasant. While the available information on an audience might not be so readily available for those not serving in public office, due diligence is easily achieved with the Internet.

- *Prepare written materials for use in the meeting.* While a lobbyist will not want to drown the Members and staff they meet in paper, concise "leave behinds" are important to conducting an effective meeting. Typically these are one- to two-page summaries of the issue at hand and any proposed legislative or regulatory solution. These materials will usually be drafted together with the client and may involve weeks of research and editing. Printed PowerPoint slide decks that include maps, charts, and other illustrations may be useful for the lobbyist or client executive to guide the discussion. Likewise, a brief agenda or simple slides will keep the focus on you and your message during a presentation. Leave behind material that requires heavy reading. Distinguish between the agenda you need for the audience to follow the meeting and the materials or slides you want to leave behind so your message can be reinforced. Use a bullet-point agenda because there's less risk that the audience reads ahead or is distracted.

- *Research and understand the underlying issue.* Lobbyists in the course of representing a client and advocating on behalf of the client's positions or favored legislative proposals will certainly develop an understanding of the relevant law and policy. In the cases of new issues, the lobbyist or lawyer in any situation will certainly want to research the topic to be conversant and responsive to questions during the meeting.

8.5   Working in Groups

More and more—especially at larger firms where matters are "bigger"—the practice of law is a group event. Of course, there are still practice and team leaders and first and second chair and a pecking order on who gets to handle the good stuff and who gets the dribble. It's hard sometimes for the associate to get the spotlight of a presentation so she can gain experience or shine. My advice to the partners—you have to give them stage time if you want to help them develop good oral communication skills. My advice to the associates—you have to seize every opportunity and create your own low-cost opportunities to practice your skills. If you cannot get on the stage at work, take the acting lessons I recommended earlier in chapter six.

Volunteer for pro bono work. Get into a leadership role in a church or community organization.

The group has changed. Changed patterns of immigration over the last few decades and fewer barriers to education have opened doors to a greater variety of attorneys, professionals, and managers at businesses. Different ages, genders, races, and viewpoints provide benefits to the legal profession. Diversity increases collaboration, and collaboration requires teams to work more effectively. If you haven't embraced diversity, perhaps the bottom line will encourage you. Clients seek diversity because their customers seek diversity. Most audiences expect diversity—or at least a diversity-sensitive lawyer.

Don't think that just because you fall within an identified minority group that you can ignore this section. Most of us are the minority or majority at one time or another. Knowing how to present with diversity in mind can be the key to keeping clients happy.

One way to increase your odds of diversification is to deliver a group presentation. Presenting as a team increases the odds that the audience will identify and appreciate someone in your firm or government division. Learning how to present well within a group increases everyone's likability factor because group dynamics become exciting and effective, not duplicative and contentious.

Not only will group presentations help show the diversity of your team, but group presentations show an audience instant collaboration techniques. A smooth group presentation displays a spirit of cooperation and team-building, often missed by lawyers. Presenting effectively together requires you to accomplish the following goals.

8.5.1 *Work with Guided Collaboration*

Presentation teams work best when headed by a gentle monarch. Appoint a leader to guide the group and make final decisions. A good leader who keeps the group focused on the super-objective will enhance the brainstorming efforts of a group.

8.5.2 *Identify the Best Role for Everyone on a Team*

The attorney with the relationship with the client might serve the team best as a "master of ceremonies." The expert on a particular provision in the code might need to deliver the explanation to the attorney general that the new legislation costs the state more money than expected. Identify the best role for each team member and wholeheartedly dive into your role.

8.5.3 *Rehearse*

Everyone has a busy schedule. To improve, the team members must commit to practice and give honest, constructive feedback. Once you devote yourself to a rehearsal time, keep the appointment and arrive prepared. Ask a nonteam-member group to offer feedback during a rehearsal, so you can fix troublesome areas before prime time. If you know that tensions are high within a group, ask an unbiased colleague to watch the presentation and provide helpful feedback for all the presenters in the group. That way, group members avoid criticizing each other—the last thing needed to build consensus.

8.5.4 Create Win-Wins by Trusting and Supporting Your Colleagues

Sometimes it can be hard to collaborate after years of climbing the ladder of success. When competition between colleagues steals the show instead of meeting the needs of the audience, everyone loses. To avoid infighting, build trust and support during a presentation. Audiences drink it up. Trust within a professional group is built on knowing that your colleagues 1) want the best for you and 2) will do the necessary work to follow through with their piece of the presentation. Each member of the group must participate and deliver. Work hard to give your entire group a sterling reputation of excellence, and help one another when someone falls short.

If you know from past history that a core group of attorneys present together (pitches, presentations, teaching, persuading superiors, reporting), schedule time to collaborate, identify talent and weaknesses, rehearse, and begin to trust each other's strengths. Also be proactive in lending a hand to bolster the team's weak areas. Here are some brief instructions to form a small group.

Form a Small Group Exercise

Form a group of attorneys to develop oral communication skills and facilitate ongoing personal development for each attorney. Once the attorneys have been divided into small groups, meet at least once a month to practice presentation techniques discussed in the book (voice and speech pattern, body language, emotion). These meetings are intended to help the attorneys work together and collaborate on improving the effectiveness of oral communications. Please find below suggestions for helping you organize small group sessions:

- Elect one attorney to serve as a scheduling coordinator, whose responsibilities will include 1) organizing the group meetings at a mutually agreeable time for all small group members, 2) reminding the members what the focus of the presentation will be for each session, and 3) sending reminders to the attorneys. Each meeting should last one hour.

- During each sixty-minute small group meeting, each attorney should be prepared to deliver a thirty-second personal description or a three- to five-minute description of a matter for a client presentation.

- After each individual presentation, make sure that the group member critiques focus on the goal at hand. Each audience member (the non-presenting members of the group) should strive to provide one suggestion and one compliment to the presenter. Track progress for each presenter and set goals for the future.

- Spend the balance of each hour discussing best practices in delivery and ongoing business development.

These tips are suggestions. The ultimate goal is for each small group should use their time together to collaborate and improve.

Chapter Nine

Litigator Track

"True eloquence consists in saying all that is fit to be said, and leaving out all that is not fit."

—La Rochefoucauld

9.1   Meeting the Bar

The audience in litigation—the judge, jurors, opposing counsel, client, even a criminal defendant—expects an Academy Award performance when an attorney stands up in court. Henry Fonda, Gregory Peck, Meryl Streep—and even Joe Pesci—set the bar high. There is no way around this expectation. We've all seen too many movies and TV shows. It's a fact. Most litigators don't dazzle the audience—and wouldn't ever be considered for an Academy Award nomination. This is true even when the attorney knows his or her case inside out. The problem is that most attorneys lack the oral presentation skills needed to fully persuade, to dazzle, to win.

I repeatedly hear judges at all levels talk about their disappointment with the bad communication skills of litigators. Litigators are expected to enjoy and have mastered the art of persuasion. Audiences demand a litigator to have a commanding voice, charismatic presence, and smooth body language. With the bar so high, even the most talented speakers need to train and prepare to meet and hopefully exceed expectations.

Knowing your own style and setting measurable goals will help you improve and adapt your presentation style as needed. Being prepared thoroughly is more than knowing your case inside and out, having fully researched and effectively briefed the issues. If you have to open your mouth in court, in a meeting in chambers, or on the phone, you are not ready if you have not invested in honing your oral presentation skills generally and specifically for the presentation at hand.

Train and improve constantly and consistently. As long as actors who play lawyers continue to improve their craft, so must you. The performance tools to improve voice, body language, and emotion must be part of you, and you must constantly expand your toolbox. Most of the techniques needed to constantly meet the growing performance expectations of the population are included earlier in this book. This chapter highlights specific areas of concern to litigators. Certain basic foundations help craft great performances in litigation.

9.2   Pretrial

9.2.1   *Identify the Theory of the Case*

Having a legally correct and persuasive theory of the case is the overarching reason why you win the war. Decide it early and develop your arguments around the theory of the case (e.g., Mrs. Simpson was wrongly accused).

9.2.2   *Know Your Super-Objective for Each Task*

For each presentation, identify a clear super-objective (win the motion or protect the client in the deposition). In the case itself—and the battles along the way—there will be super-objectives, such as arguing a motion or taking a deposition. Within each super-objective, develop specific themes so you can present your arguments in a clear and concise manner.

9.2.3   *Tell a Story*

You must distill your case—civil or criminal—into a simple, understandable, and in the end, believable, story. As facts present themselves, and the story starts piecing together during the client interview and discovery period, begin a frame board or PowerPoint slide for each event. This headlining technique helps design a beginning and ending for each action sequence, making it easier for you to tell and recall a compelling story once you know all the facts. For example, if you are litigating an insurance claim, a frame or snapshot from a piece of your story may look like the following:

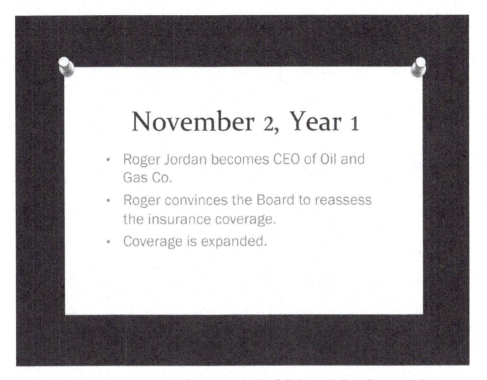

Eventually, you can use the frames or deck of slides to help tell a story that starts by grabbing the attention of the listener and ends by summarizing the issues and requesting a call to action.

9.2.4 *Explain the Process to Your Client*

Clients consistently complain about litigators failing to communicate the process clearly or keeping the client informed as developments happen. Take steps to give clients a visual picture of things to come. Develop and use a linear timeline, with date ranges, to keep clients informed. A simple example is provided below.

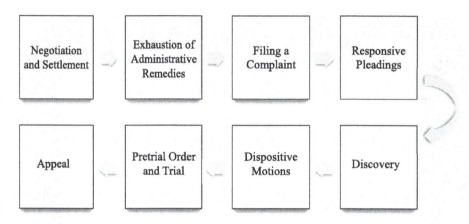

9.2.5 Develop Your Client to Be an Advocate for His Own Case

Even if the client never speaks during a trial, arbitration, or mediation, his non-verbal performance matters. The client must have a clear understanding of theory of the case, the themes you will use the develop that theory, the overarching super-objectives as well as the super-objective of the task at hand, and the path to achieve those super-objectives. Remember that the client is also one of the actors on the stage during litigation, and she needs to play her supporting role at the same high standard. Weave your super-objective and themes into the timeline and explain the process with the goals intertwined.

9.3   Trial

During a jury trial, teach the jurors the terms of art you will be using (hopefully only a handful). Use these teaching moments to bond with the jurors, and craft your instruction in a way that makes the jurors feel smart. Use visual aids—create (or assign someone to create) a log of possible visual aids that can be used later in depositions, pretrial, or trial. Professor Peter Lyons, an international specialist in advocacy and dispute resolution suggests:

> As counsel, your job is not just to argue the case or to represent your client as well as you can. There is a higher duty. You should aim to assist the court in coming to the conclusion that suits your client. Assisting the court means being credible. Credibility is born of honesty and competence and a comfortable familiarity with the case and the law. Assisting the court means speaking slowly and clearly, in short phrases and with just the right amount of passion. It means being interested in what you are saying and conveying to the court that you are there to help. With a judge you must show that you are there to help them make or

even write the decision. With a jury it is making them feel that you are working out the problem with them.

Devote the time needed to practice every oral presentation. In general, set aside one hour of prep for every ten minutes of presentation.

Never ignore the body language of the judge or jurors. One of the most important skills you can acquire as a litigator is reading body language. You need to remain alert to the verbal and nonverbal cues the judge, jurors, and opposing counsel give. Often, you will need another set of trained eyes in the room to observe the nonverbal cues. In addition to a sharp legal mind, this observer needs a keen understanding of the super-objective and themes. This "observer model" also works outside the courtroom in business meetings. When you are presenting, you tend to focus on one particular audience member or group; a trained observer can use the feedback she gleans from silent observation to guide the presentation to success. If you use the observer model, schedule regular breaks so you can hear that feedback and adapt accordingly.

9.4   Handling Difficult Audiences as a Litigator

If you practice law as a litigator, you choose a field of law that lives and breathes tension. The client arrives in a mess both physically and emotionally, and you need to clean him up. If a company faces litigation, long gone are the honeymoon days of a business deal's beginning. If spouses seek good litigators, it means divorce is on the line. Prosecutors and defense attorneys argue their cases to punish or set free. Litigation is costly and wrought with high stakes.

Sometimes the tension brings out the worst in people—even you. A good litigator needs to manage difficult personalities, including his own, with fine-tuned oral communication skills. That difficult personality might be co-counsel, opposing counsel, the judge, the client, an expert, or a witness. Learning how to keep your composure and avoid being drawn in emotionally to the drama of an offensive individual is one key to success. However, you will often need to "act" to control or manage the path forward. Some guidelines follow.

9.4.1   Establish and Maintain Relationships

If you build a reputation for handling the combative nature of litigation, a deviation from your norm will be taken in context. Consistent, cool-headed behavior prevails in the end. After controlling the nerves and settling your brain around the task at hand, relationships take over. Work on establishing a relationship by getting to know your audience and then connecting with that audience. Focus on making good eye contact, imbuing your voice with a warm tone, keeping emotional control, and creating well-planned gestures. You may have a different relationship with each of the players—client, judge, opposing counsel, associate.

Continually maintain presence and poise (and only lose it when it is for a purpose that supports a theme or the super-objective). Your goal should be for you to be known for your poise under pressure. You may need to ignore some belittling comments. If offensive behavior reaches a level of disgust or makes it difficult to represent your client well, address it. If you are in a room full of people and someone is disrespecting you, it often helps to keep your focus (eye contact and voice projection, body direction) on the decision-maker in the room. Focus all comments, even about the offending individual, at the decision-maker in the room. If possible, repeat back the offensive language, comment, or tone for the record. By focusing on the decision-maker and entirely ignoring the person lobbing attacks your way, she may eventually bury herself by looking unreasonable and out of control. There are other tools that you can deploy when appropriate in these situations. I caution that there is risk in too bold or aggressive a response.

9.4.2 Pick Your Battles

Ignoring difficult personalities is often your best avenue to success. This is especially true when the difficult personality is your co-counsel, client, or the judge. If you think confrontation is necessary, choose those moments sparingly and deliver the message with deferential physical behavior and a measured volume in your voice.

Recognize when you might be the natural target of combative people. For anyone in law school or just beginning a legal career, remember that you are more likely to be taken advantage of when you are young and inexperienced. Presenting yourself with confidence reduces the potential abuse to you and your client. Regardless of experience, if you act scared, some individuals will walk right over you. A certain amount of bravado is necessary to prevent being disrespected. So how can you practically do that? Try pushing back against a combative audience with certain techniques.

Sometimes disrespect comes from a lack of manners or an irreverent title. I often hear young female associates tell of war stories of opposing counsel trying to belittle them by calling them "Honey" or "Sweetie." Quickly put an end to such behavior by requesting such name calling to stop. There are unique and humorous ways to do this, but they have risk. Remember Ronald Reagan in an early debate when his age was being raised as an issue against his election—he responded that he "would not make an issue or allow others to make an issue an issue of his opponent's youth and immaturity." We are not all blessed with Reagan's style.

If repeated bad behavior occurs, switch communication to written form to keep a record.

9.4.3 Choose Strategies that Make You Appear and Sound Confident

Keep a broad posture, project your voice, lower your pitch, slow down your speed, and increase your use of pauses.

Staying in control helps you appear more confident. Only get agitated if you choose to be agitated. Choose to be agitated only to move a theme forward or get closer to the super-objective. An aggressive attack is difficult to continue if no resistance is given. Eventually the attacker implodes from the lack of force coming from the other side.

Practice all presentations, including phone calls, in stressful environments—don't practice a difficult cross-examination alone in the comfort and safety of your office. Practice with distraction, noise, the unexpected, and a cantankerous participant (in a small room with young children—your own or borrowed—after a long, rainy indoors weekend, for example). Simulate a stressful situation in which to practice so the real performance seems effortless.

9.5 Dealing with Juvenile Clients

Many of my clients tackle intense pro bono work from time to time. These cases tend to involve juveniles, and I often receive questions about how to represent child-clients more effectively. These cases are often wrought with emotion, so maintaining composure and professionalism becomes challenging. As a juvenile's representative, appearing in control and in command is critical. As Professor Michael J. Dale knows from a lifetime of service to juveniles, "The more professional the lawyer, the more the child is taken seriously." Keep things professional to maintain your objectivity.

As you prepare communications with your juvenile client, keep the content simple. Rely on analogies and timelines to explain outcomes and process. Figure out how your client understands information best. Use visual and auditory senses to help your client retain information. These same rules should be followed in dealing with many adult clients.

Some attorneys think that a juvenile client can only understand things if communicated in a "baby voice." Avoid changing your natural pitch because it sounds artificial and condescending. If you want to connect, focus on maintaining eye contact and slowing down your speed. Keep in mind that juvenile clients may have less physical self-awareness. This may manifest as a hypersensitivity to an invasion of their personal space or a lack of respect for your personal space.

9.6 Dealing with Different Audience Sizes and Formalities

Litigators should train for varied levels of formality and audience size. Sometime a litigator needs to walk the factory floor to interview a witness. Sometimes she argues before an appellate judge or a three-judge panel. Sometimes the audience is the trial judge, and sometimes it's the members of the jury. Sometimes when you are addressing the judge, the intended audience is a witness or the jurors. Know who you are really talking to. Whether in a two-hour hearing, an afternoon in court, or a day-long deposition, you have to be prepared to effectively use the elements of style—voice, body language, and emotion—to achieve the super-objective. This requires you to transition in and out of the formal and casual settings and in and out of different audience sizes.

The different levels of formality and audience size require you to be flexible. A good litigator is persuading in every moment—coming in and out of a place, transitioning to and from different audiences. You need to be able to make quick and accurate adjustments to your style.

One of the first skills to sharpen is the ability to listen actively. For a litigator, this can become a powerful tool of persuasion. If you can master active listening, reacting with facial animation and body language cues, you can lead audiences like juries or judicial bodies to see things your way. They begin to empathize and tag along your emotional journey—build a little pathos. One way actors succeed at active listening is by pretending to hear answers for the first time. Avoid the temptation to fall asleep during your own directs and crosses because you heard the answers a hundred time in preparation. Stop looking at the paper and connect with the human on the other end. Another actor exercise is to repeat back answers, lobbing words back and forth with different emotions each time. This repetition game helps you remain a learning listener, staying present in the moment. It allows you to stay in the role, even when you aren't center stage. Active listening keeps audiences watching the listener and his reactions.

Sometimes you want to self-direct your reactions so that the judge and jurors see that you aren't fazed at all by something revealed at trial. Staying deadpan and unsurprised lessens the impact of a deadly comment for your client if you show no reaction. Again, it's controlling the flexibility of your presentation style. Overfocusing on something makes you look uneasy about the revelation.

Staying flexible during a presentation also helps as you shift from small audiences to large audiences. For a litigator, this can happen within seconds. One moment you address a jury of many, and the next moment you address a witness directly. Even though the fact-finder continues to be your audience, your body position changes focus from the witness (one person) to the jury (larger group). To succeed with the audience size change, you must be able to expand and contract the intensity and grandness of your style to remain suitable for the space and audience.

Think of your body language as an accordion, expanding and lengthening when the audience grows in number and contracting in size and scope when the audience size shrinks. When the audience increases in size, you increase your stylistic elements. Bigger voice volume, bigger facial expressions, bigger gestures, slower tempo, more expressive energy for a big audience. For a smaller audience, shrink the elements in size and intensity.

9.7   Dealing with the Noncommunicative Client and the Needy Client

Oral presentations don't happen only when you stand up in court. Every time you are with our client, you are making an oral presentation. And these types of presentations can be critical. You need to use the skills we've talked about to have success with a client. I find that non-communicative clients either need more silent windows to speak openly or generally need help making decisions. If you have a noncommunicative client, try speaking less and—something that might be more difficult for you—being comfortable with mutual silence. Sometimes the client becomes more comfortable speaking when you stop. Ask questions that are hard to answer with a simple "yes" or "no." Ask specific questions that invite a monologue, then request details.

Some clients are genuinely bad at making decisions. Use your oral presentations skills to lead them. Timelines, deadlines, and decision charts can be your lifeline to reaching them. After giving them limited options, establish reasonable times for them to reach decisions. Help them understand the consequences of decisions by visually helping them see the result of going down a certain rabbit hole.

For the needy clients out there—the ones who call all the time and suck the very life out of you—set up healthy boundaries early on that allow you to work efficiently. Tell such a client: "I will reserve the four o'clock hour just for you every day for us to touch base. That way, I can report developments and keep moving the ball forward on your case during the day." Don't make the mistake of telling the client that you are working on someone else's matter. No client likes to hear that they hold second place on your priority list.

If the client is truly a clingy monster, establish body language that divides the space. You're your shoulders squared and sit with ample space between you. Defer to phone calls where you can remove yourself more easily than an in-person meeting. Try getting a third party to buffer the communication flood. Setting up a system of healthy communication boundaries from the beginning often avoids the entanglements of a needy client.

9.8   Representing an Unlikable Client

Clients are not always likable. As the attorney of an unlikable client, you must show the audience that you represent your client with pride. When that feeling of admiration is hard to muster, especially in court or arbitration, try the following exercise to bend your mind around a more cheerful representation.

Toast Your Client Exercise

1. The ultimate goal of the "Toast Your Client Exercise" is to improve your tone in court as well as represent your client professionally in an oral presentation with the right tone. A good way to start is to take a friendly toast and convert it to an introduction in a formal arena. Imagine yourself at a wedding reception or a banquet. You have been asked to raise a glass and give a toast for your client. This toast should start by giving a brief background of how you know the client and then continue with the reasons why you enjoy representing her. Here is an example:

    > Steve Apple and I met at a charity event in Los Angeles seven years ago when he first started making widgets. Since then, he has provided me with a steady income, exciting legal work, and constant telephone calls.

2. Now keep the same emotional tone you used to make the social toast above and change the text to the opening of a motion in court. Here is an example:

    > Your Honor, my name is Rebecca Diaz-Bonilla, and I represent Steve Apple. My client seeks Summary Judgment.

3. Practice varying your tone until you reach the perfect attitude for the specific presentation at hand. Practice in the extreme, since your nerves will shrink the progress you make in the actual performance.

CHAPTER TEN

COMMUNICATION ISSUES FOR WOMEN

"This above all: to thine own self be true."

—*William Shakespeare*

10.1 Perspective

For many years, I have been asked to speak with groups of women lawyers. Topic requests range from how to succeed on a call or in a meeting, to networking techniques, to challenges associated with work-life balance. I usually begin with a few disclaimers—which are also necessary to start a chapter devoted to issues that specifically challenge women lawyers:

1. *In this chapter, I address only the habits and tendencies that are stereotypical for women.* I have to generalize to draw conclusions and make recommendations. For example, men generally have a 15 percent larger body frame than women. Men generally have deeper voices than women. There are, of course, many women with deep voices and tall frames that break the stereotypes, but I will not address every exception to a rule. That is more efficiently and appropriately done through individual coaching. If I lecture to a group of women about communication rules based on stereotypes, then I use a quick individual coaching meeting to tell the lawyer what rules to break based on her individuality. For purposes of this chapter, I will generalize.

2. *I celebrate the differences between men and women.* I think it would be quite a boring world if we were all the same. And while I believe that best practices of communication speak to any audience, I happen to enjoy the different powers of communication that are typical to men and typical to women. I have no interest in a cookie-cutter world.

3. *Lawyers should treat others, and should expect to be treated, justly.* I think reward should be based on merit, and a lawyer should be valued because of her ability, not because of her gender. I personally strive to be valued and become indispensable because of my abilities, which are enhanced by the nuances of my femininity, not because I am a token diversity number on a project.

4. *I am a believer in taking action instead of whining.* I feel incredibly blessed to live in a time and place where I am free to achieve my goals. I have generations of men and women throughout history to thank for those rights and privileges. When an injustice exists for a man or woman, I believe in finding a solution. I was raised to wake up each morning and acknowledge that I owe the world my very best instead of thinking that I am owed. Because of all my privileges, I have a duty to improve the lives of women and men.

5. *Resurrect the virtue of modesty.* Keep private things that should remain private. We are living in a time of oversharing. I have noticed the most successful female lawyers not only dress professionally and smart, but also avoid telling someone information they do not have the right to know. The next time you have to take a child to a doctor's appointment, try saying, "I have an appointment," instead of "I have to take my child to a doctor's appointment."

6. *Find a mentor and a champion.* The best mentor relationships I see exist between two professionals who never actually work on a project together. A mentor should be someone you can confide in and from whom you can receive work advice without fear of evaluation. A champion, on the other hand, is someone who works with you who will lobby for your advancement.

7. *Control the tone in emails.* Try not using qualifiers or unnecessary apologies, use full sentences, be polite, be professional. Drop the exclamation points.

With those disclaimers in mind, let's get started.

10.2 Succeeding as a Female Lawyer

The majority of a lawyer's oral communication happens in calls and meetings today. To develop new habits, these delivery genres provide the most practice time available to cement change. The table below outlines typical tendencies between men and women.

Women	Men
Higher vocal register and lower volume	Lower vocal register and higher volume
Undervalue their own strengths	Overvalue their own strengths
Smaller physical stature	Larger physical stature
More perceived upspeak	Less perceived upspeak
Seek consensus	Seek win
Low interruption pattern	High interruption pattern
Intros – fate happened	Intros – "I" happened

This chapter will cover these issues, put into the context of various scenarios.

10.3 The Basics

Here is a list of communication best practices that I look for in all advocates, but find women are more challenged to accomplish competency in certain areas.

- Deliver a confident introduction.
- Project your voice.
- Speak without fillers, qualifiers, and upward inflection (upspeak).
- Make appropriate eye contact.
- Smile.
- Energize your posture.
- Use effective gestures.
- Show enthusiasm and warmth.

10.3.1 Deliver a Confident Introduction

Here are some good steps to building a confident introduction to be used in short version during a networking event, meeting, or call, or in long version for a pitch or other business development event.

1. Write your rank (i.e., years in practice and practice area), three bullet points describing your professional practice, and what makes you unique as a lawyer.

2. Edit the language to use active verb choices. This changes your introduction from sounding like "fate happened to me" to "I happened." For example, "I try to help clients . . ." versus "I help clients . . ." or "The firm asked me to join . . ." versus "I joined the firm to . . . ."

3. Edit the language to switch team-oriented language to the first person. You can always add it back and give credit where credit is due, but women sometimes don't give themselves enough credit for accomplishments. For example: "The regulatory practice build its FCC client based after many years of becoming the experts in town," versus "I became an expert in FCC law and my client base grew as a result."

4. Practice anecdotes or examples to illustrate your bullet points to be used during small talk.

10.3.2 Project Your Voice

Females have higher registers, which can be more difficult for audiences to hear, especially over the telephone. In addition, certain cultures encourage women to keep volume lower than normal to appear more docile and respectful. When audiences cannot hear you, they will tune out. When you speak too loudly, audiences will be annoyed or perceive that you are shouting at them. Properly projecting your voice is essential for basic communication success.

There are objective ways to measure your decibel levels, and I encourage you to use those technologies. But technology isn't always readily accessible in a meeting with colleagues, not to mention how awkward it would look to conduct a meeting while externally and publicly measuring decibel levels. The best way to discover if you are properly projecting your voice is to ask: "Please let me know if you can't hear me in the back of the room." If an audience member ever tells you he cannot hear you or to "speak up," you must deliver.

The adjustment of volume should happen with the diaphragm, as discussed in Chapter Four, "Voice/Speech Basics—Posture, Breath, Sound, and Quality." Once you've practiced changing your volume and adjusting volume, you will develop muscle memory and better regulate your volume based on the acoustical needs of the setting. Noticing when to adjust volume is critical, and we need to watch for non-verbal cues to help us know when to dial up or down. The table below outlines a few nonverbal cues to look for to know whether to turn up or down your volume. You should take in a combination of these context clues and pivot in the moment.

Turn It Up	Turn It Down
Audience asks basic questions covering topics clearly covered	Audience is reluctant to ask any questions
Audience breaks contact completely and stops listening (checks cell phone or reads material)	Audience moves or shifts away from you
Audience facial expression shows frustration, confusion, strain, or boredom	Audience facial expression shows pain or annoyance
Audience speaks to you in an overly projected voice	Audience speaks to you in an overly quiet volume

10.3.3 Speak Without fillers, Qualifiers, or Upward Inflection

I have sad news to report: I hear upward inflection and fillers in both male and female voices. Fillers become more problematic for women when they already have stylistic tendencies that undermine their confidence. For example, when a woman has a voice that is thin in quality and low in volume, and then adds repetitive fillers ("um," "ah," "er") to the speech pattern, this becomes the perfect vocal storm.

I am often asked, "Is the perception that women have higher rates of upward inflection just an unfair stereotype?" My response: "No." Women's voices are naturally higher in pitch, so a listener will be alerted to an upward inflection used by a woman more readily than by a man. With that in mind, I find it more important for a woman to curb upspeak to achieve the perception of confidence.

Many female lawyers have a propensity to reduce the power or directness of their communication by clogging their phrases with qualifiers: "I just," "like," "you know," "sort of," to name a few. If we are searching for a confident and likable style, try smiling more during a greeting section and reduce the qualifiers.

Delivered with a warm, professional smile: "Hello. I have a strategy to share with you today."	To	Delivered with a stoic expression: "So, like hello. I would just like to take a few minutes of your time today to sort of explain a strategy for you."

10.3.4 Make Appropriate Eye Contact

My concern for women regarding eye contact relates to culture-specific norms that encourage women to overly guard eye contact or avoid direct eye contact. This casting down of the eyes may be a successful and possibly necessary cultural trend in certain countries, but American audiences look for strong and direct communicators. Looking someone in the eye in America also delivers a sense of credibility and honest dealing, essential elements of the good Aristotelian ethos discussed in this book.

I recommend that women who have to succeed in different cultures learn how to master the habit so they can employ the right technique at the right time. If you find yourself in a culture that appreciates less eye contact, learn to adjust your eye contact contention time and practice breaking eye contact and focusing on notes or the substantive gestures[1] you are making. When you shift back into the Western culture, connect with direct eye-contact focus for a few seconds at a time and build endurance.

10.3.5 Smile

The most powerful and confident speakers whom I've had the privilege to coach use expressiveness as a leadership tool. They are emotionally in tune with the words and phrases expressed, and their facial expression matches those messages. They cue the audience to follow their lead when they smile or frown, and instruct the audience as to how they should feel about a particular section. It is powerful.

I find many women unfortunately think that erasing their personalities and neutralizing facial expression will make them appear confident and demand to be taken seriously. They are grossly misguided. Being expressive is a powerful tool of communication, and it is far easier to reduce the intensity of expressiveness than to create emotion out of nothing. When a communicator stays stoic on the wrong

---

1. See Chapter Five, "Body Language."

section or phrase—for example, "Welcome to the annual conference on world policy"—the speaker looks nervous or angry or untrustworthy. Not confident.

If you are not a practiced user of proper facial expression, get a mirror and use it at your desk during phone calls. You can train your facial muscles to awaken and start working to support your message instead of being a distraction.

10.3.6 Energize Your Posture

Since women generally have a smaller physical frame, we have to compete for eye attention. It's not the 6'5" linebacker-sized man's fault that every eye looks his way when he walks into a room. He is probably used to visual attention being sent his way. Women have to compete with those body types. We can do this by picking home bases that broaden our shoulders and widen our horizontal stance. We can avoid crumbling our posture and build muscle strength at our core to keep posture animated and engaged. If you find yourself using body posture that makes you look bored or disengaged, roll back those shoulders and take up more space.

10.3.7 Use Effective Gestures

There must be some terribly trained, archaic, chauvinistic teacher in almost all the pasts of my female clients who told them that they should not gesture when they are speaking in a professional setting. This phantom teacher must be stopped. The female lawyers who have heard this lie deliver for what seems like an eternity in complete stillness. Often, I see a muscle twitch or try to disobey and move. The moment they finish and conversation commences, these women slip into a natural and winning gesticulation pattern. They are interesting and clear and expressive. Sure, sometimes they need to control the number or size of gestures, but I prefer genuineness. So please, erase the voice of that teacher from long ago and use gestures.

10.3.8 Show Enthusiasm and Warmth

I meet many female lawyers who think that to compete in a male-dominated workforce they have to evaporate enthusiasm—"I can't look young and peppy"—and warmth—"People won't listen to me if I'm friendly and warm." I acknowledge that women have a narrower band of accepted emotional expression, but I encourage all women to show variation and be pleasant, warm, professional, and passionate about their work. These emotional layers are additional tools for you to employ, and you need to use them at the right time. There is no perfect dose of any emotion. We all come into a situation with a childhood, wounds, and successes. Some of us are introverts, and others are extroverts. Be yourself and avoid hiding genuine and effective facets of you. Being polite and warm will generally win you more rewards that punishments. I tell clients to notice and register how they behave with people who are family or friends with whom they feel a freedom to be themselves. Notice how you relate to those loved ones, with openness within your own bandwidth of expressiveness. Bring elements of those facets into the workplace and dial them down as needed . . . just don't erase them altogether.

I recognize the need for women to appear confident and should look like they should be taken seriously. Think of your stylistic adjustments to reach the right balance much like an equalizer sound system. If you stop upward inflicting, start using more natural and warm facial expression. As you properly project your voice, use more polite language choices with lots of "please" and "thank you." Find a balance that works for you.

10.4 Change the Mindset

I was recently prepping a female client for an important interview. We were focused on the techniques for answering a "difficult personality" question. You know the drill: "Tell me about a difficult client you have had" or "How do you handle difficult personalities?" As I covered the reasons why government agencies, firms, or in-house counsel may ask interviewing lawyers such a question, my client grimaced at a key part of my explanation:

> Jane, this GC may ask you about how you deal with difficult personalities, and for good reason. First, they are checking to make sure *you* are not the difficult personality. Second, they want to see if you have developed a healthy layer of Teflon to handle a lot of stressed-out people who solve big problems. Third, they are seeing if you are reasonable and give people the benefit of the doubt. Are you litigious-happy? Can you tell the difference between stressed assertiveness and abuse? Do you give people a break when they have a bad day or week or month? Fourth, do you recognize that there are many ways to solve conflict? Sometimes, ignoring bad behavior is the best response. Other times, stopping it in its track makes sense. At times, you need to paper your communication and take a "wait and see" approach. And when it's abusive, you need to tell someone what's happening.

If you guessed the first, second, third, or fourth point as to when my client grimaced, you would be correct. She flinched at every single one. I find these visceral reactions are common among my female outplacement clients. My explanation of a fairly typical interview question sparks quite different nonverbal reactions from men. I am not suggesting that the men's reactions don't worry me, because they do. Let me explain what I've discovered from unpacking these female reactions again and again.

1. *They are checking to make sure you are not the difficult personality.* Jane's grimace during this point speaks to a tendency for female lawyers to undervalue what they bring to the table. A lot of women think they are always the difficult one in a work relationship. This perspective comes with lots of second-guessing themselves, and this sometimes bleeds into doubting the quality of their work.

   Other women think about the many work relationships that were sour but which they tried endlessly to make pleasant. This perspective can happen when a woman is trying to make something social out of something that is just fine remaining sterile and even cold. Yes, there are times when a woman's natural ability to be relational comes in handy as a lawyer. But there are many times in law and business, when clients and colleagues want a lawyer who can be an emotionless surgeon. No friendship is desired, and no warm fuzzies are needed to achieve success . . . just quality work for a fair price. This model of lawyering can be tough on men and women, but I see women more unable to embrace a sterile relationship devoid of small talk, niceties, and smiles. A colleague of mine recently heard I was coaching a client who was known for being extremely difficult to manage. This client would bark at you for breathing too much of his air. This colleague asked how I had managed to deal with him. I replied, "Well, he has thus far treated me with respect, and I'm learning so much from his brilliance. But I am a tool for his success, a means to an end, and I won't let myself or him forget that. I'm good with that."

Adopt a necessary, optimistic outlook on situations and find the value beyond the relationship. Keep in mind that rank rules the room. The client or your supervisor sets the emotional tone of a relationship. You can nudge around the edges, but the one in charge should decide the tone of the engagement. Look and listen for context clues. If a work colleague or client speaks curtly or fast-paced, make certain you are listening to the total message delivered. When someone needs to get off the phone quickly but says "thanks," trust that all is well.

2. *They want to see if you have developed a healthy layer of Teflon to handle a lot of stressed-out people.* People make mistakes. Mistakes, even outbursts, happen once in a while to everyone. Patterns are quite a different situation. Most lawyers deal with stressful situations and issues. Being a lawyer can be trying. To survive and thrive, you will need to develop an ability to let things roll off your back. I was in a strategy meeting for a difficult regulatory matter. The senior partner had a cross facial expression, methodical pace, and strained vocal tone. His stylistic delivery matched the tense circumstances perfectly. As I walked out of the room with a female colleague, she complained about how mad and distant the senior partner seemed during the meeting. I was shocked. Taking that stress personally or expecting someone to trivialize the situation with frivolity seemed totally inappropriate to me. She responded to me: "He is always like that. He has never wanted to develop a friendship with me."

To succeed and not take things personally, I suggest distinguishing between friendships and work colleagues. Not everyone you work with is destined to be a friend. There are people who have personal boundaries that are more narrow than yours. Respect other people's different approach.

Realize that cultural and familial circumstances exist that don't interfere with the quality of the work.

3. *They are seeing if you are reasonable and give people the benefit of the doubt. Are you litigious-happy? Can you tell the difference between stressed assertiveness and abuse?* Many women are suffering from a crisis of over-sensitivity and under-sensitivity to perceived or real mistreatment. A good rule of thumb to follow is to give other people the benefit of the doubt. Extend the courtesy of good intentions to them unless that interpretation would be unreasonable.

4. *Do you recognize that there are many ways to solve conflict?* Problem-solving skills should extend to interpersonal relationships. When someone's behavior is challenging, avoid an emotional reaction and explore all strategy options available to you. This skill will be handy when you need to separate emotion from a client matter.

   When dealing with a difficult personality, sometimes ignoring bad behavior is the best response. Other times, stop it in its track and then let it go. At times, you need to probe or paper your communication or wait and see. And when it's bad, you need to tell someone what's happening. Speaking up about an abusive relationship is a duty. It prevents others from future mistreatment from an aggressor.

10.5 Analyze Communication Patterns

We develop patterns of communication throughout time, and certain patterns shape audience perceptions of us. I find that when female lawyers monitor and utilize apology, saying "no," and interruption patterns, they appear more confident and in control. For all these patterns, try these steps for improvement.

1. Observe the pattern used by your team, and specifically by the leadership or client. If you are on a team that rarely interrupts, then your interruption pattern may need to be reduced to match the tone of the group.

2. Track your pattern. Becoming self-aware is one of the most valuable communication improvements and can be particularly helpful in these pattern alterations.

3. Recognize that to shift an impression of you that has already been set based on past behavior requires more exaggerated correction. If you've been reluctant to interrupt until now, you'll have to really put yourself out there to move the impression needle in the other direction.

4. Ask for team feedback, and if necessary, permission. At your next feedback moment with a team member, tell them your plan. "I've noticed that I over-apologize for things, and I'm determined to stop. I think it's undermining my authority with the client. Can you listen and let me know if you hear any improvement?"

10.5.1 Adjust Your Apology Pattern

Some people naturally apologize more frequently than others. Perhaps, if you are like the Fonz on *Happy Days*, you can't even mutter the words "I'm sorry." I hear women over-apologize for things outside their control. If you make a mistake for something you were responsible for, then by all means, apologize. If it was not your responsibility or was outside of your control, avoid it. Sometimes we need to fill our word bank with some replacement phrases to fix this bad habit.

Mistake Done Within Your Control and You Are Responsible	Mistake or Bad Luck Not Within Your Control and You Are Not Responsible
"I'm sorry."	"I'm sad to hear that."
"My bad."	"What a disappointment!"
"Please forgive me."	"That should not have happened."
"This was my responsibility, and I messed up. Please give me another chance."	"I understand why you are frustrated, and I would be if I were in your shoes."

10.5.2 Sometimes Say "No"

If you've rarely said "no" to an incoming assignment and realize you aren't doing a high-quality job on projects, you may be stretched too thin. If you are committed to working a certain amount of hours every day, then work smarter by having the courage to give yourself enough time to complete work properly. When possible, say "no." I know this is hard, but it can change your practice. Including responses to requests that communicate "no" can be hard to implement. Practice.

Say "No" When Needed
"I would like to be on this project, but I would not be able to get you that memo until ___."
"I just committed to a new assignment that's taking up all my time. I'm not able to do that this week."
"I can complete this for you, but I would need to bring someone else on board for the short term to help get you these things right away. Does that work?"
"I can't get that done for you within that time frame."

10.5.3 Interrupt Properly

There is an art to interruption. Rank rules the room. Interrupting someone senior to you should only be done sparingly. Interruptions in general are usually poorly done and turn into hijacks instead of interruptions. It's important to practice the right "why" and "how" of interruptions.

Why? Interruptions are appropriate when:

1. You are correcting a logistical mistake: "Jim, I'm sorry to interrupt. There is a newer version of that document. Let me send it over now."

2. You are asking a necessary question: "Sally, excuse me for a moment. Did Judge Black issue the order? We couldn't hear you."

3. You are contributing a value-add: "Hank, pardon the interruption, but have you read the latest stats on this? They will change the outcome . . . ."

How? To avoid hijacking the conversation, follow these steps:

1. Say the name of the person speaking. This is especially important on a conference call with many dial-ins. If you are in a live meeting, you can physically signal the speaker that you are interrupting.

2. Apologize. Interrupting is rude, and politeness demands a quick apology. Avoid groveling or taking too much time.

3. Project your voice so you are heard clearly.

4. State the reason for the interruption, and then stop or pass back the baton.

Finally, once you become indispensable as a lawyer, advocate for yourself. Spend your time at work contributing and developing into a valued and necessary team member. Only after that quality is established is advocating for advancement appropriate. More often than not, I see men advocate for themselves more readily than women. Voice concerns and ask for what is fair. All the strategies and observed best practices mentioned in this chapter should be utilized to practice law successfully and courageously. Instead of masking our personalities and femininity, why not find strength in them?

Chapter Eleven

Parting Advice

"I will let the facts speak for themselves."

—*Demosthenes*

The pressures of a legal practice can feel overwhelming. You are pulled from all sides. Now I have added another load for you to carry—building in time to improve your oral communication skills.

You have learned an array of strategies in this book to help you improve different areas of oral communication—preparation, voice and speech pattern, body language, and emotion. Sometimes you need to create opportunities to practice your oral communications skills—pro bono cases, training younger lawyers, adjunct teaching positions. Despite the best intentions, the reality of a busy practice and personal life makes doing all of the exercises in this book difficult. So here are some shortcuts or ideas to help you get by.

11.1 Prioritizing in Practice

Even if you consistently work on improving oral communication skills, occasions arise that require an immediate response. You are faced with quick deadlines, so knowing how to prepare when short on time is critical. What should you do first? How do you prioritize?

Begin with the bookends: appearance and substance. On the one end, like it or not, most people take you more seriously if you dress in a tidy and professional manner. And on the other, if you speak with compelling force, but your message is weak, you will not convince the audience. Clients, judges, and colleagues expect you to deliver substantive and sound advice.

Once you've taken care of those extremes (the superficial shell and the heart of your presentation), fill in the middle (i.e., improve the delivery) with basic techniques. Start with confident posture, good volume, appropriate eye contact, gestures that put the audience at ease, and a good rate of speed suited for the audience's understanding.

The key is preparation—even if you have no time to prepare. Here is my prescription for how to prepare within different time frames and the order of operations to put your best foot forward in any presentation. When faced with a compressed practice time, try out these prioritized systems to avoid feeling overstressed and out of time.

Five Minutes to Prepare

Preparing the Presentation	Voice and Speech Pattern	Body Language	Emotion
One minute— • think about the presentation • set super-objective and themes *One minute—* • outline the presentation in bullet point format	*One minute—* • practice the first thirty seconds of your opening • project your voice and eliminate upward inflection	*One minute—* • check your appearance and tidy yourself • align posture • practice a commanding starting home base	*One minute—* • concentrate on feeling confident and persuading the audience • practice achieving your super-objective

Thirty Minutes to Prepare

Preparing the Presentation	Voice and Speech Pattern	Body Language	Emotion
Five minutes— • think about the presentation • set super-objective and themes, with specific memorable "headlines" for each theme you choose *Five minutes*— • outline the presentation • if appropriate, create a short agenda for the audience	*Ten minutes*— • practice the first three minutes of the presentation and the closing three minutes • practice projecting your voice • speak without an upward inflection • avoid fillers ("uh" or "ah") • alter speed depending on your tendency to go too fast or too slow	*Five minutes*— • check your appearance and tidy yourself • align posture • practice specific home bases and opening gestures for the first three minutes	*Five minutes*— • decide a specific emotional intention for each section of your bullet point outline

One Hour to Prepare			
Preparing the Presentation	Voice and Speech Pattern	Body Language	Emotion
Five minutes— • think about the presentation • set super-objective and themes with specific memorable "headlines" for each theme you choose	*Ten minutes—* • practice the first three minutes of the presentation and the closing three minutes • practice projecting your voice • speak without an upward inflection • avoid fillers ("uh" or "ah") • alter speed depending on tendency to go too fast/slow	*Five minutes—* • check your appearance and tidy yourself • align posture • practice specific home bases and opening gestures for the first three minutes	*Five minutes—* • decide a specific emotional intention for each section of your bullet point out outline *Five minutes—* • practice an exaggerated friendly opening

One Hour to Prepare—Continued			
Preparing the Presentation	Voice and Speech Pattern	Body Language	Emotion
Five minutes— • outline the presentation, and if appropriate create a short agenda for the audience • fill outline with supporting points and arguments	***Ten minutes—*** • using your bullet point outline, practice aloud the first minute of each section of your presentation • practice a crisp vocal delivery as mentioned above for the opening and closing ***Five minutes—*** • using your bullet point outline, practice the transitions between sections • say aloud the last sentence of each section and move to the beginning of the next section.	***Five minutes—*** • practice the home bases transitioning from one section to another	

Sometimes you can carve out practice time in unexpected ways, so be creative with how you squeeze in prep time. For example, try writing out your presentation until you settle into language and themes that you like. Try reading those sections into your smartphone recording application. Listen to the recordings while you commute or travel to commit the phrasing into memory.

Keep track of improvements while you prepare. When I meet with clients, I use review sheets to compare and track improvements. Use a form like this one to track your own improvements.

Graphics	
Substance	
Voice Quality	
Speech Pattern	
Gestures, Posture	
Facial Expression	
Tone/Emotion	
Audience Connection/ Eye Contact	
Dynamic Levels	
Improvement Recommendations	

11.2 Job Interviews

Interviews scare a lot of people. Interviews can make or break our next career move or educational opportunity. The primary way to improve your interview success is to prepare and practice. Prepare the right message, and practice the presentation techniques necessary to make a great impression. Preparation is directly proportional to success. Here are a few job interview tips that are sometimes forgotten.

11.2.1 Have Your Personal Introduction Down Cold

Your thirty-second and three-minute introduction of yourself should be well written, memorized, and rehearsed. Record these introductions and listen back until you have honed it with compelling wordsmithing and effective delivery.

11.2.2 Attend to Your Dining Manners

If you have never been taught proper meal etiquette, pick up a book on manners (or go home for a refresher). There are shocking stories about bright attorneys and law students who destroy their chances of employment because of embarrassing table manners. At the very least, chew with your mouth closed, avoid slouching, and be sociable (i.e, avoid talking about yourself too much; instead, engage others, ask questions, and get to know them). Eating together is a way for employers to see if you would work well together and enjoy each other's company.

11.2.3 Determine the Employer's Need and Fill It

If you want to fill the needs of your audience, you must find out more about them. Research the employer and be brave about asking the human resources representative to give you a better sense of what kind of attorney the organization is seeking. Even though questions are being asked of you, control the interaction by delivering a planned message through the answers. Highlight experiences that set you apart, but avoid listing hundreds of accomplishments—especially if they are already on your résumé. The interview provides the opportunity to share what is not written on the CV. In the interview, determine the right ethos, logos, and pathos to meet the needs of the employer. Practice for the interview with those goals in mind.

11.2.4 Network

Like it or not, knowing someone helps. Create a running list of contacts and develop those relationships. Reach out to contacts and ask for information and a good recommendation. Good networking requires consistent maintenance and creative links from contact to contact. Investment now will reap benefits in the future. If you consider yourself a poor networker or the efforts involved in networking are distasteful to you, practice. Force yourself to put down your smartphone and converse with colleagues. Get to know the people you encounter, starting with your innermost circles, then working out from there. You'll find that you know more people than you think and that everyone wins with genuine networking efforts.

11.2.5 Control the Message

When preparing for an interview, don't practice until you've crafted the themes you want to leave with the interviewer. Rehearse ways to weave in your messages through the question-and-answer format. Have a friend or colleague run a mock interview to practice returning to your strongest reasons why you should be hired.

11.2.6 Connect with the Interviewer

Ask questions about the firm or company that can't be found on the website. Listen to the answers and maintain good eye contact. Keep your body language energized and your posture aligned. Remember that most interviews occur with one or two audience members, so avoid distracting or fidgety gestures. Project your voice a degree more than you think necessary and enunciate. Nothing kills an interview when the audience cannot understand your words. Watch for the reactions of the interviewer and respond accordingly. Avoid looking down at the floor or flashing shifty glances. Stay focused on the interviewer and be enthusiastic about the questions asked.

11.3 Using Handouts and Visual Aids

Handouts and visual aids can be a wonderful tool or a killer to a presentation. Learning how to manage a handout and visual aid widens your scope of possibilities as a presenter. Here are a few suggestions from years of coaching.

11.3.1 Introduce Handouts in the Beginning to Wrap-Up Housekeeping Items

Take a moment to give people a quick tour of the handout. Not only will it help you push through the initial adrenaline rush, but it also helps you stay in command of the room. It's better to guide them through this exploration of material while controlling the event. If you don't explain the handout, they will ignore you and your presentation while they look at the material. Tell them how to use the handouts and whether you want them to use the material during the presentation. If there is no purpose for them to have the material during your presentation, wait to hand out the documents until after you finish the presentation.

Decide whether handouts would help or hurt your presentation. Handouts allow the speaker to include more text than a properly prepared PowerPoint allows. Handouts can be used to 1) help the audience take notes and 2) show detailed statistics, case law, or studies that you reference in the presentation. Sometimes a handout can simply be an agenda for the meeting, which gives the audience a clear roadmap of what to expect. If you believe your presentation needs a handout, create one that moves the ball forward.

11.3.2 Use Visual Aids to Keep the Audience Interested in the Presentation

PowerPoint, flip charts, and whiteboards can liven up a presentation. Use these visual aids interactively. The slides provide an outline for the speaker and the audience. Having graphics or a whiteboard helps focus the audience's attention. Incorporating the visual component to the presentation helps the audience learn and retain the content. Keep slides simple and free of wordy text. You want the audience to pay attention to you, not puzzle out the wall of text.

Wait until you establish stardom before using visual aids. When using Power-Point or other visual aids, memorize the opening and closing of the presentation. Delivering the first few minutes without notes and without the slides alerts the audience that you have control of the room and that the slides are supporting you, rather than you using the slides as a crutch. In general, stand to the side of the screen, positioning your body toward the audience as much as possible. If you want the audience to stop looking at the slides, step in front of the presentation. You can also cross in front of the presentation to address questions from the audience. If necessary, read the screen text, then add your commentary.

Learn how to incorporate the visual aid by gesturing towards the current point. That way you draw the audience's eye towards the point at hand. If you write on a board while speaking, either finish writing and turn to speak or amplify your volume while you write so the audience hears a continual decibel level of sound.

11.4 Lessons Learned and Reinforcement

Improving your oral communication skills will be a lifelong journey. Aim for logical solutions to roadblocks along the way. I recently coached an attorney who described being extremely nervous despite being adequately prepared. I asked him where he was practicing and replied, "In my office." To which I responded: "Well, if the actual performance stresses you out, it sounds like you need to practice in a more stressful environment. Visit the room where you will present. Practice messing up, tripping in front of everyone, and stumbling on words. Go home and turn on the television so you have to speak over the sound and avoid the distraction of your favorite show. Ask a colleague to pepper you with rude interruptions and demanding questions. Create a stressful environment so the actual performance feels like a relief."

Find creative ways to practice your skills. If your law practice doesn't lend itself to ample opportunities, try teaching, join groups in your area that focus on public speaking, create a small group of colleagues to practice presentations, or record yourself performing and review it. If you hold a position of leadership in your office, provide opportunities for younger attorneys to speak on phone calls and meetings so that you develop their oral communication skills along with their writing skills. In doing so, you will also get a refresher course in your own abilities. The best way to thoroughly learn something is to teach it.

The power of persuasion arms you with the ability to compel audiences. In closing, remember Aristotle's formula for success: ethos, logos, pathos. Practice law with integrity so your ethos precedes you. Prepare your presentation with simple, powerful, and logical points. Inspire the audience with your voice, body language, and emotion.

It's never too late to begin improvement. If you are a gifted orator with a love of rhetoric, you can achieve even greater heights by developing your natural talent. If you suffer from a fear of public speaking, you can steel your nerves and become an effective speaker. If you are like most attorneys—with an average amount of talent, but a genuine drive to deliver—the essential techniques of oral communications skills will transform you into a lawyer who can persuade any audience.

INDEX